Living
30 Minute Meals

Best wishes

from Brifld

Living
30 MINUTE MEALS

SARA BUENFELD

HAMLYN

NOTES
Standard level spoon measurements are used in all recipes.
1 tablespoon = one 15ml spoon
1 teaspoon = one 5ml spoon

Both metric and imperial measurements have been given in all recipes.
Use one set of measurements only and not a mixture of both.

First published 1992
Hamlyn is an imprint of Octopus Illustrated Publishing,
part of Reed International Books Limited,
Michelin House, 81 Fulham Road,
London, SW3 6RB

A catalogue record for this book is available from the British Library

ISBN 0 600 57451 2
Produced by Mandarin Offset
Printed and Bound in Hong Kong

CONTENTS

INTRODUCTION 7

EVERYDAY EATING 8

VEGETARIAN MEALS 26

LIGHT AND SUMMERY 42

SUPPERTIME 58

FOREIGN FAVOURITES 76

ENTERTAINING 92

INDEX 110

ACKNOWLEDGEMENTS 112

INTRODUCTION

However much you enjoy cooking there will always be occasions when you want a good meal *fast*. Perhaps after a late night in the office; when friends drop in unexpectedly or before going out for the evening. But whatever the occasion, if you've 30 minutes to spare you'll never need to resort to 'junk' food again. Good, healthy and delicious meals *can* be achieved with the help of these menus, all of which were created exclusively for the food pages of Living magazines.

There are fast family meals for every day, romantic menus just for two - even an informal supper party for twelve - each photographed and with a helpful order of work so that everything is ready and on the table exactly as planned. Whether you fancy chicken, fish, meat or a vegetarian meal there's plenty of variety and choice using recipes inspired from all around the world.

To ensure your success all the recipes have been thoroughly tested in the Living kitchen to guarantee that they are easy to cook and taste every bit as good as they look in the photographs.

I hope you enjoy them.

Sara Buenfeld
Living's Food and Drink Editor

WARMING WINTER MEAL

Treat the family to a really warming supper
with this delicious lime flavoured chicken dish and hot banana dessert

*Chicken with
Lime and Thyme*

Garlic Vegetable Medley

Caribbean Bananas

CHICKEN WITH LIME AND THYME

Serves 4
560 Calories a portion

4 boneless chicken breasts
1 tbsp olive oil
50g (2oz) flaked almonds
1 onion, sliced
225g (8oz) long grain rice
2 limes, grated rind and juice
pinch of saffron strands
2 tbsp clear honey
2 tsp fresh thyme leaves
6 cardamom pods, crushed
2 tbsp sultanas
700ml (1.¼pints) boiling chicken stock
salt and freshly ground black pepper
small sprigs of fresh thyme, to garnish (optional)

Heat a large frying pan, add the chicken skin side down and cook until brown. Turn over and quickly seal the other side.

Remove the chicken from the pan and set aside.

Add the oil and almonds to the pan and cook, stirring until starting to brown. Add the onion then cook for 2-3 minutes more.

Stir in the rice until coated in the oil then add all the remaining ingredients and season well. Return the chicken breasts to the pan.
Cover and simmer gently for 15-20 minutes until the rice and chicken are both tender.

Garnish with the thyme before serving if liked.

GARLIC VEGETABLE MEDLEY

Serves 4
65 Calories a portion

175g (6oz) broccoli
4 sticks of celery, cleaned
25g (1oz) ready made garlic butter
or 25g (1oz) butter mashed with
1 clove crushed garlic

Cut the broccoli into small florets and finely slice the celery. Melt the butter in a large pan with the garlic, if using, and add the vegetables. Cook, stirring, for 5 minutes, then cover the pan and cook gently for a further 2-3 minutes before serving.

CARIBBEAN BANANAS

Serves 4
180 Calories a portion

4 firm bananas
25g (1oz) butter
25g (1oz) brown sugar
1 small orange, grated rind and juice
large pinch ground cinnamon
large pinch ground nutmeg
50ml (2fl oz) dry sherry
TO SERVE:
150ml (¼pt) Greek yogurt

Peel and halve the bananas lengthways then place in a baking dish.

Put the remaining ingredients in a small pan and bring to the boil. Simmer for 2 minutes then pour over the bananas in the dish.

Bake in the oven at 190°C (375°F) gas 5 for 15-20 minutes. Serve with Greek yogurt spooned over.

ON YOUR MARKS. . .

● *Put the kettle on for the boiling chicken stock*

● *Make the lime and thyme chicken. Cover the pan and leave it to finish cooking*

● *Slice the bananas and place in a dish, pour over the glaze and put in the oven to cook*

● *Prepare and cook the vegetable dish*

● *Serve and eat the first course while the banana dessert finishes cooking*

Liven up chicken with a hint of tangy lime - then follow with a mouthwatering hot banana dessert

MICROWAVE MEAL

If you find cooking a complete meal in the microwave something of a juggling act, try this delicious three-course menu

STUFFED MUSHROOMS EN CROÛTE

Serves 4
280 Calories a portion

40g (1.½oz) butter
4 slices brown bread
4 large flat mushrooms, wiped
and stalks trimmed
8 thin slices of German salami
100g (3.½oz) round goats' cheese,
rind removed, cut into 4
GARNISH:
4 walnut halves
ground paprika, for sprinkling
sprigs of parsley, to garnish

Slice the butter onto a large plate and melt on Full Power for 1 minute.

Cut rounds from the bread using a 7.5cm (3in) pastry cutter. Coat them in the butter on the plate and cook on Full Power for 2 minutes, turning them over halfway through. Transfer to a plate and leave to crisp.

Put the mushrooms on the buttered plate, then top each with 2 slices of salami and a slice of cheese. Cook, covered, on Full Power for 3 minutes until the cheese has melted. Place on the croûtes and garnish with the walnut halves, paprika and parsley.

MONKFISH WITH MUSTARD SAUCE

Serves 4
375 Calories a portion

2 skinned and boned monkfish
tails weighing 675g (1.¼lb)
(ask your fishmonger to do this)
2 tbsp lemon juice

freshly ground black pepper
1 bayleaf
MUSTARD SAUCE:
125g (4oz) butter
2 egg yolks
3 tsp Dijon mustard
3 tsp whole-grain mustard

Trim the fish into even-sized fillets and arrange in a shallow round dish. Add the lemon juice, pepper and bayleaf. Cover and cook on Full Power for 5 minutes, turning the fillets if necessary halfway through cooking. Leave to stand while making the sauce.

Slice the butter into a small bowl and cook on Full Power for 1 minute until just melted.

Whisk in the egg yolks, 2 tablespoons of fish juices and the mustards. Cook on Full Power for about 30-40 seconds, whisking every 15 seconds, to mix the mustard and make a smooth butter sauce. Taste and season if necessary.

Drain the fish fillets and arrange on a warmed platter. Spoon the mustard sauce to cover. Serve the remaining sauce separately.

SUMMER CABBAGE

Deseed and slice a red pepper into thin strips and cook on Full Power for 2 minutes, with 15g (½oz) butter, in a large covered bowl. Mix in 175g (6oz) each finely sliced white cabbage and Savoy or green cabbage. Sprinkle with 2 tablespoons lemon juice then cover and cook on Full Power for 4-6 minutes, stirring halfway through. Drain and toss before serving.

These recipes were tested in a 600 Watt microwave.

HOT NEW POTATOES

Place 450g (1lb) washed small even-sized new potatoes in a large bowl with 4 tablespoons water. Cover and cook on Full Power for 8 minutes, stirring twice.

Leave to stand for 5 minutes then drain and add 1 tablespoon each of walnut or olive oil and freshly chopped spring onions. Season well then cover and cook on Full Power for 2 minutes more until hot.

PLUMS IN RED WINE

Serves 4
100 Calories a portion

2 tsp arrowroot
2 tbsp water
75ml (3fl oz) red wine
1 tbsp Amaretto di Saronno
(almond liqueur), optional
8 large, ripe red plums, halved
and stoned
2 tbsp demerara sugar
ratafia biscuits, to serve

Blend the arrowroot with the water in a measuring jug. Whisk in the red wine and cook on Full Power for 1-2 minutes, whisking twice, until the sauce has thickened and cleared. Add the liqueur if using.

Arrange the plums, cut side down in a dish, prick the skin using a sharp knife. Pour the sauce over the fruit, sprinkle with sugar, then cover and cook on Defrost for 6-8 minutes until the plums are just soft. Leave to stand and cool for a few minutes.

Spoon the fruit and sauce into 4 sundae glasses and top each with ratafia biscuits to serve.

*Stuffed Mushrooms
en Croûte*

---

*Monkfish with
Mustard Sauce*

Summer Cabbage

Hot New Potatoes

Plums in Red Wine

Microwave magic: clockwise
from left, Summer Cabbage,
Plums in Red Wine, Monkfish
with Mustard Sauce and Hot
New Potatoes, and Stuffed
Mushrooms en Croûte

ON YOUR MARKS. . .

- *Put the potatoes into the microwave while preparing the fish, bread rounds and the red pepper*

- *Assemble the mushrooms while the croûtes are cooking then set both aside. Cook the red pepper, shred and cook the cabbage*

- *Prepare the plums and red wine mixture, thicken the sauce, pour over the plums and set aside*

- *Cook the fish. Set aside in its juices. Melt butter for sauce and add remaining ingredients, ready to cook*

- *Put the mushrooms in the microwave to cook. Meanwhile drain the vegetables, adding the dressing to the potatoes*

- *Garnish and serve the mushrooms. Reheat the potatoes with the dressing while eating the starter*

- *Just before serving the main course, finish the sauce, arrange the fish on plates and reheat the cabbage*

- *Put the plums in the microwave to cook while eating the main course*

A SATURDAY SNACK

Saturdays *should* be relaxing – though more often than not they're a turmoil of chores and shopping. So what's needed is a quick and nutritious snack like this delicious tomato and vegetable soup served with tasty pork and sage burgers

Saturday Soup

Pork and Sage Burgers

SATURDAY SOUP

Serves 4
125 Calories a portion

25g (1oz) butter
4 medium carrots, finely sliced
(about 450g/1lb)
4 celery sticks, finely sliced
4 medium leeks, trimmed and
thinly sliced (about 225g/8oz)
400g (14oz) can chopped
tomatoes
575ml (1pint) chicken or
vegetable stock
2 tsp Worcestershire sauce
salt and freshly ground
black pepper
GARNISH (optional):
4 tbsp natural yogurt
freshly chopped parsley or spring
onion tops

Melt the butter in a large saucepan. Add the carrots, celery and leeks and fry over a moderate heat for about 5 minutes until softened, but not browned. Pour in the tomatoes and stock, add the Worcestershire sauce and season well. Bring to the boil, then cover and simmer for 15-20 minutes until all the vegetables are just tender.

Pour half the soup into a blender or food processor and purée until smooth, return it to the pan and reheat until boiling. (The soup can be served without blending, but the consistency will be thinner.)

Serve in hot soup bowls and garnish, if liked, with a spoonful of yogurt and a sprinkle of chopped parsley or spring onion tops.

PORK AND SAGE BURGERS

Makes 8
220 Calories each

450g (1lb) lean minced pork
1-2 tsp freshly chopped sage or
½ tsp dried
salt and freshly ground
black pepper
TO SERVE:
4 mixed grain rolls or onion and
rye baps, halved
4 tbsp mayonnaise
a few crisp lettuce leaves
2 tomatoes, thinly sliced
a little lemon juice
2 spring onions, chopped
sprigs of fresh sage, to garnish
(optional)

Using your hands, mix the mince with the sage and seasoning. Divide the mixture into 8 then shape into flat rounds - a 7.5cm (3in) biscuit cutter will help make all the shapes an even size. Place the burgers on foil on the grill pan and cook under a hot grill, for about 4 minutes on each side.

Warm the split rolls or baps in the oven or under the grill then spread with a thin coating of mayonnaise. Arrange some lettuce and a slice of tomato on each one then top with a hot burger. Squeeze over some lemon juice then sprinkle with the spring onion.

Serve 1-2 per person depending on appetites. Eat immediately garnished with sage and salad, if liked.

Saturday Soup served with Pork and Sage Burgers - healthy, tasty and a real change for all the family

ON YOUR MARKS. . .

- *Prepare and fry the vegetables for the soup. Put the kettle on for making the stock. Put bowls to warm*

- *Turn on the grill to heat. Make and shape the burgers. Add the stock and tomatoes to the soup*

- *Start grilling the burgers*

- *Prepare the salad and warm the rolls or baps*

- *Purée half the soup, return it to the pan and reheat*

- *Put the mayonnaise and salad on the rolls. Place the burgers on top and garnish. Ladle the soup into warmed bowls and serve immediately*

DELICIOUS MID-WEEK MEAL

Here's an excellent new idea for pork chops,
served with special noodles and seasonal fresh peaches to follow

*Pork with
Stroganoff Sauce*

*Ribbon Noodles
with Thyme*

Fruit and Nut Peaches

PORK WITH STROGANOFF SAUCE

Serves 4
345 Calories a portion

**4 boneless pork loin chops,
trimmed of fat
salt and freshly ground
black pepper
1 tbsp sunflower oil
2 onions, sliced
1 clove garlic, crushed
125g (4oz) baby button
mushrooms, wiped
1 tbsp ground paprika
2 tsp tomato purée
2 tbsp dry sherry
425ml (¾pint) chicken stock
3 tbsp Greek yogurt
2 tbsp freshly chopped parsley
TO SERVE:
225g (8oz) fine green beans
15g (½oz) butter**

Season the chops with the ground
pepper. Heat a non-stick frying pan
then dry fry the chops over a high
heat for 2 minutes on each side.
Remove the chops from the pan and
place under a low heated grill to finish cooking.

Add the oil to the pan (still with the
sediment from the meat in), then fry
the onions and garlic until softened.
Add the mushrooms and cook for
2 minutes more. Stir in the paprika,
tomato purée, sherry and chicken
stock then cook uncovered until the
mushrooms are tender and the stock
has reduced by half.

Trim the ends from the beans and
cook in boiling salted water for 5-7
minutes. Add the yogurt, parsley and
seasoning to the sauce.

Spoon over the pork chops and
serve with the noodles and buttered
green beans to complete the meal.

RIBBON NOODLES WITH THYME

Serves 4
280 Calories a portion

**850ml (1.½pints) chicken or
vegetable stock
225g (8oz) dried ribbon noodles or
tagliatelle
25g (1oz) butter
1tsp fresh thyme leaves or
½ tsp dried
freshly ground black pepper**

Heat the chicken or vegetable stock
in a large pan until boiling, add the ribbon noodles or tagliatelle (making
sure they are all covered in the stock)
then put on the lid and cook for 12
minutes or until tender.

Remove the lid and drain the noodles (although there shouldn't be
much stock left). Return the noodles
to the pan and carefully toss in the
butter, thyme leaves and freshly
ground black pepper.

FRUIT AND NUT PEACHES

Serves 4
300 Calories a portion

**75g (3oz) ground almonds
50g (2oz) hazelnuts, chopped
4 glacé cherries, chopped
1 orange, grated rind and juice
4 ripe peaches, halved and stoned
2 tbsp light brown sugar
7g (¼oz) butter**

Place the almonds, hazelnuts, cherries, orange rind and 2 tbsp of juice in
a bowl and stir together.

Spoon a little of the fruit and nut
mixture into each peach half then
place in a flameproof dish, sprinkle
over the sugar and dot each peach
with a little butter.

Place the dish under a low heated
grill and warm through until the sugar
is golden and bubbling.

TASTY LAMB DINNER

Liven up lamb chops with a delicious orange and mint baste, serve with delicate but speedy courgette and carrot ribbons, and follow with tropical fresh fruit salad

Minty Orange Lamb Chops

Courgette and Carrot Ribbons

Salad of Exotic Fruits

ON YOUR MARKS...

- *Put a pan of water on to boil for the potatoes*

- *Prepare the lamb chops and cover in the minty orange baste. Set aside*

- *Put the new potatoes on to cook and preheat the grill for the chops*

- *Slice and arrange the fruit salad on a platter. Spoon over the passion fruit seeds and pulp and chill until ready to serve*

- *Place the lamb chops under the grill to cook*

- *Prepare and cook the courgette and carrot ribbons, keep an eye on the lamb and turn over after 5 minutes*

- *Drain the potatoes and serve with the vegetables and lamb*

While cooking the chops in their minty marinade, conjure up an original vegetable dish and tropical fruit salad

MINTY ORANGE LAMB CHOPS

Serves 4
270 Calories a portion

4 lamb chump chops, trimmed of excess fat
1 tbsp olive oil
1 tbsp green pepper jelly (see Cook's Note)
1 tbsp Dijon mustard
3 tbsp chopped fresh mint
1 orange, grated rind and 4 tbsp of juice
freshly ground black pepper
TO SERVE:
450g (1lb) new potatoes, scrubbed

Put a pan of salted water on to boil for the potatoes. Prick the chops all over with a fork and place them in a shallow dish. Mix together all the remaining ingredients, pour over the chops, then toss them until they are covered in the baste. Set aside until 10 minutes before serving. Put the potatoes on, cook for 20 minutes.

Place the lamb chops under a preheated grill and cook for 5 minutes each side until golden on the outside and pink inside. Serve with the drained new potatoes.

COOK'S NOTE
Green pepper jelly is now becoming available from more and more supermarkets and specialist delicatessens, and it has a wonderfully pungent flavour. If you can't find it, substitute the same quantity of redcurrant or blackcurrant jelly or soft brown sugar.

COURGETTE AND CARROT RIBBONS

Serves 4
40 Calories a portion

2 large courgettes, washed
2 large carrots, peeled
15g (½oz) butter
freshly ground black pepper

Cut the courgettes and carrots in half crosswise, and using a vegetable peeler slice off thin ribbons down the length of the halved courgettes and carrots.

Heat the butter in a non-stick frying pan and add the courgettes and carrots ribbons. Stir fry for 1-2 minutes. Grind some black pepper over the vegetables before serving with the lamb.

SALAD OF EXOTIC FRUITS

Serves 4
75 Calories a portion

4 kiwi fruit
1 mango
8 fresh dates
2 passion fruit

Peel the kiwi fruit, then cut across in thick slices. Cut through the mango lengthwise 1cm (½in) from each side of the centre to remove the flat stone. Peel the two halves and slice the flesh. Peel and cut off any mango left on the stone. Halve and stone the dates.

Arrange the fruits on dessert plates. Halve the passion fruit and scoop the seeds out onto the arranged fruit. Chill.

SPEEDY MID-WEEK MEAL

Impress everyone with this special mid-week meal: everyone will be fooled into thinking you've spent hours in the kitchen

TROUT WITH TARTARE BUTTER

Serves 4
350 Calories a portion

75g (3oz) butter, softened
1 tbsp capers, roughly chopped
1 cocktail gherkin, finely chopped
2 lemons
1 tbsp freshly chopped parsley
four 225g (8oz) whole trout, cleaned
salt and freshly ground
black pepper
French bread, to serve

Mix the butter with the capers, gherkins, the grated lemon rind of one lemon and the parsley. Shape the butter into a sausage, wrap in greaseproof paper and freeze for 15-20 minutes.

Cut slits in the trout and place on a grill pan. Slice the remaining lemon and place inside the fish. Season the trout well and place under the grill for 6-7 minutes each side, or until the flesh flakes easily when tested with the point of a knife.

Slice the butter into 8 thin slices and serve on top of the trout.

Serve any remaining butter separately with the vegetables or spread onto the French bread and serve with the meal.
Not suitable for freezing.

BRAISED MIXED VEGETABLES

Serves 4
40 Calories a portion

300ml (½ pint) vegetable stock
150g (5oz) broccoli spears
125g (4oz) thin asparagus tips
125g (4oz) mangetout, tailed
25g (1oz) flaked almonds, toasted
salt and freshly ground
black pepper

Heat the stock in a large pan until boiling, add the broccoli, cover and cook for 2 minutes. Add the asparagus and cook for 3 minutes more then finally add the mangetout. When tender drain the vegetables and toss in the flaked almonds. Season to taste.
Not suitable for freezing.

MOCHA CREAM

Serves 4
300 Calories a portion

50g (2oz) plain chocolate
75ml (3fl oz) double cream
4 tsp brandy
300g (11oz) fromage frais
2 tsp coffee and chicory essence
(Camp Coffee), or 2 tsp
coffee granules dissolved in 2 tsp
boiling water
1.½ tbsp caster sugar
wafers, to serve (optional)

Place the chocolate and cream in a small pan and heat very gently until the chocolate has melted. Add the brandy and stir well to make a chocolate sauce. Set aside.

Mix the fromage frais with the coffee and chicory essence and the caster sugar.

Pour a little of the chocolate sauce into 4 glasses (it doesn't matter if it's still warm). Top with the coffee mixture and marble the two mixtures together before serving.

Serve topped with crisp ice cream wafers if liked.
Not suitable for freezing.

Deliciously simple - trout with a tangy tartare butter and braised mixed vegetables, then smooth Mocha Cream

Trout with Tartare Butter

Braised Mixed Vegetables

Mocha Cream

ON YOUR MARKS. . .

- *Heat the grill and toast the almonds for the vegetables. Make up the coffee if not using essence for the dessert. Allow them both to cool*

- *Make the tartare butter and put in the freezer to chill*

- *Prepare the fish and cook under a medium grill for 7 minutes on each side*

- *Put the vegetable stock on to*

boil while preparing the vegetables

- *Add the vegetables to the stock. Turn the trout over and leave to cook on the other side*

- *Make the chocolate sauce and coffee cream for the desert*

- *Drain and serve the vegetables with the trout and tartare butter Marble the mocha dessert just before serving*

COLOURFUL STIR-FRY SUPPER

Hungry and in a hurry? Stir-fry this tasty mixture of mustard marinated lamb, leeks, broccoli and potatoes and follow with a zingy fruit dessert

LAMB AND APRICOT SAUTÉ

Serves 4
475 Calories a portion

1 tbsp clear honey
1 tbsp dark soy sauce
½ tbsp whole mustard seeds
2 tsp ready-made English mustard
450g (1lb) lamb fillet, cubed
12 no-need-to-soak dried apricots
2 tbsp oil
2 large potatoes, scrubbed and cut into sticks
2 leeks, sliced
225g (8oz) broccoli, divided into florets
1 tsp cornflour

Mix together the honey, soy sauce, mustard seeds and the made mustard. Add the lamb and apricots then leave for a few minutes to marinate.

Meanwhile, heat a tablespoon of the oil in a large non-stick frying pan, add the potatoes and cook gently, stirring occasionally, until golden on all sides. Meanwhile, heat the remaining oil in another pan. Add the meat and apricots, reserving any marinade, and stir-fry until the meat browns. Add the leeks and broccoli. Cover and cook for about 10 minutes until the meat and vegetables are tender. Mix in the potatoes. Transfer to a hot serving dish. Blend the cornflour into the reserved marinade then add to the pan juices, heat, stirring until thickened.

Pour over the meat and vegetables and serve.
Not suitable for freezing.

BLACKCURRANT AND RASPBERRY REFRESHER

This is very quick to prepare and makes a lovely fruity end to a meal. Adding the frozen raspberries to the hot blackcurrant mixture means that you don't have to wait for them to thaw, and at the same time they help to cool the dessert.
Serves 4
65 Calories a portion

1 tbsp cornflour
300g (10oz) can blackcurrants in natural juice
225g (8oz) frozen raspberries
1-2 tbsp caster sugar
4 sprigs of mint, to decorate (optional)
raspberry fromage frais, to serve

Blend the cornflour into a little water, add to the blackcurrants in a pan and heat gently until thickened.

Remove from the heat, add the frozen raspberries and sweeten to taste. Set aside and leave to cool. Then chill until ready to serve.

Divide between dessert glasses, decorate with the mint if liked and serve with the fromage frais.
Not suitable for freezing.

Lamb and Apricot Sauté

Blackcurrant and Raspberry Refresher

ON YOUR MARKS...

- *Mix the marinade ingredients together for the lamb sauté, add the cubes of lamb and apricots then set aside*

- *Make the blackcurrant and raspberry dessert then leave to cool*

- *Chop up all of the vegetables for the lamb dish, heat the oil in two separate pans then start to cook the potato sticks in one and the meat and vegetables in the other*

- *Transfer the dessert to serving dishes and put in the fridge to chill until ready to serve*

- *Toss together the sauté potatoes and the meat and vegetables, thicken the pan juices with the cornflour then serve immediately*

Delicious and simple - Lamb and Apricot Sauté followed by Blackcurrant and Raspberry Refresher

SPRINGTIME DINNER FOR FOUR

A bright, colourful and fresh-tasting menu for four – just right for spring!

Pork Argenteuil served with Buttered Pasta

PORK ARGENTEUIL

Argenteuil is the French name for a dish using asparagus.
Serves 4
255 Calories a portion (without pasta)

25g (1oz) butter
1 onion, sliced
500g (1lb) pork fillet, cut into
16 slices
1 tbsp flour
½ tsp chilli powder
salt and freshly ground
black pepper
250g (8oz) frozen asparagus, cut
into 2.5cm (1in) pieces (see
Cook's Note)
125g (4oz) button mushrooms
½ orange, grated rind and juice
3 firm tomatoes, each cut into
6 wedges

Melt the butter in a large frying pan and cook the onion for 3 minutes over a moderate heat. Meanwhile dip the pork slices in the flour seasoned with chilli, salt and pepper. Move onion to one side of the pan.

Add the pork slices and cook for 2-3 minutes each side to brown the meat. Sprinkle in any remaining flour. Mix the onions with the meat and add the asparagus. Place the mushrooms on top, cover the pan and cook for 5 minutes.

Stir in the orange rind and juice and place the tomato wedges on top. Cover and cook for 2 minutes for the tomatoes to warm through.

TIMEPLAN FOR SERVING DINNER AT 7.30PM

7.00 *Prepare the rhubarb and start it cooking. Chop the onion.*
7.05 *Cook the onion and coat the pork slices in seasoned flour, add to the frying pan. Cook for 2-3 minutes each side.*
7.10 *Add the blended arrowroot to the rhubarb, bring to the boil and add the raspberries. Pour into a serving dish.*
7.15 *Put the kettle on for water to cook the pasta. Cut up the asparagus and add to the pork*
with the mushrooms. Prepare orange rind, juice and tomatoes.
7.20 *Put the pasta on to cook in a large pan of boiling salted water for 5 minutes. Add orange rind, juice and tomatoes to the frying pan. Swirl Greek yogurt or cream into the Kissel.*
7.25 *Drain the pasta and toss with lemon wedges and parsley butter. Transfer pork and vegetables on to a warmed serving dish.*
7.30 *Serve main course.*

Transfer pork and vegetables on to a serving dish and serve with fresh pasta tossed with parsley butter and lemon wedges.

COOK'S NOTE
If you're able to buy fresh asparagus, scrape off any hard woody parts from the stems, trim then cut into 2.5cm (1in) pieces. Cook for 5 minutes longer, before adding tomatoes, until tender.

RHUBARB AND RASPBERRY KISSEL

Fresh, young rhubarb heralds the start of the red fruits season. Marry with easily obtained frozen raspberries and a dash of almond essence and you have a simple but sophisticated dessert – delicious served warm or cold with thick yogurt or cream. Kissel is a dessert of Russian origin, made from tart fruits.
Serves 4
60 Calories a portion (without biscuits)

500g (1lb) fresh, young rhubarb, cut into 2.5cm (1in) pieces
8 tbsp fruits of the forest juice (see Cook's Note)
2 tsp arrowroot
few drops almond essence
250g (8oz) frozen raspberries
2 tbsp Greek yogurt or cream, for decorating

Put the rhubarb pieces in a pan with 6 tablespoons of the fruits of the forest juice. Cover the pan and simmer for about 6 minutes until the rhubarb is just soft.

Blend the remaining 2 tablespoons of juice with the arrowroot and almond essence, mix into the rhubarb, bring to the boil, then stir in the raspberries. Pour the fruit mixture into a serving dish and leave to cool a little.

Just before serving, lightly swirl yogurt or cream through the fruit.

COOK'S NOTE
Grenadine syrup can be used instead of the fruits of the forest juice, use diluted by half. Check the sweetness and add brown sugar or honey if necessary. For a special occasion, use Amaretto (almond liqueur) instead of almond essence.

WINE CHOICE
The best drink to complement Pork Argenteuil is Normandy cider: try any fairly dry cider, still or sparkling according to preference. Or try a dry but fairly robust white or rosé wine from Provence, or a blush wine from California. Rhubarb is a difficult fruit to partner, but more Amaretto liqueur will match, or a Vin Santo (strong, sweet white wine) from Italy, or a medium dry Madeira such as Verdelho.

Pork Argenteuil

Buttered Pasta

Rhubarb and Raspberry Kissel

Rhubarb and Raspberry Kissel - a type of compote

SPECIAL FAMILY MEAL

Serve this steak supper for your next family celebration

Steaks with Peppercorn Sauce

Hot Potato Salad

Broccoli

Exotic Fruit and Chocolate Platter

STEAKS WITH PEPPERCORN SAUCE

Green peppercorns in brine taste quite different from dried black peppercorns. They have a fresh spicy flavour which combines well with meats like beef steaks, lamb and pork.
Serves 4
351 Calories a portion

15g (½oz) butter
4 beef or lamb steaks
1 tbsp crushed green peppercorns
150ml (¼pint) chicken stock
3-4 tbsp Greek yogurt

Melt the butter in a large frying pan then fry the steaks over a high heat to seal each side.

Turn down the heat, add the peppercorns then cook until the steaks are cooked to your taste. Remove from the pan and place on a warmed serving platter.

Add the stock to the pan and boil rapidly, stirring to incorporate all of the pan juices. Remove from the heat then stir in the Greek yogurt. Pour over the steaks and serve immediately with broccoli florets.

HOT POTATO SALAD

Serves 4
150 Calories a portion

Boil 500g (1lb) small whole new potatoes for about ten minutes or until tender.

Meanwhile finely slice two small red or ordinary onions, cut four tomatoes into wedges and finely chop some parsley until you have 4 tablespoons. Place in a salad bowl with 175g (6oz) baby button mushrooms and 2-3 tablespoons of Italian or French dressing.

Drain the potatoes, add to the other ingredients and serve.

EXOTIC FRUIT AND CHOCOLATE PLATTER

Treat yourself to a selection of exotic fresh fruits and wafer thin chocolates when there's simply no time to prepare a dessert.
Serves 4
220 Calories a portion

1 paw paw, sliced
2 kiwi fruit, halved
small bunch of grapes
125g (4oz) lychees
125g (4oz) chocolate thins

Arrange the prepared fruit and chocolates on a serving platter or cake stand. Chill until ready to serve.

TIMEPLAN FOR SERVING THE MEAL AT 7.30PM

7.00 *Prepare the Exotic Fruit and Chocolate Platter. Cover and store in the fridge until ready to serve.*
7.05 *Put two pans of salted water on to boil. Prepare the broccoli and wash the potatoes and put on to boil.*
7.15 *Rinse the button mushrooms, quarter the tomatoes and slice the onions.*
7.20 *Start to cook the steaks with peppercorns. Meanwhile chop the parsley and add to the salad ingredients with the dressing.*
7.25 *Drain the broccoli and potatoes. Arrange the broccoli on a large platter. Toss the potatoes into the salad. Arrange the steaks on the platter with the broccoli.*
7.30 *Add the stock and yogurt to the pan juices then spoon over the steaks and serve.*

Steaks with Peppercorn Sauce and broccoli, Hot Potato Salad and Exotic Fruit and Chocolate Platter to follow

VEGETARIAN LUNCH

Fast, tasty, *and* it's suitable for vegetarians – fresh pasta tossed in a rich cheese and tomato sauce and served with a crisp salad of different leaves. For dessert, enjoy passion fruit scented peaches and Amaretti biscuits

Fresh Tagliatelle with Cheese and Tomato Sauce

Leaf and Nut Salad

Peaches with Passion Fruit

FRESH TAGLIATELLE WITH CHEESE AND TOMATO SAUCE

Serves 4
520 Calories a portion

1.½tbsp olive oil
sprig of fresh rosemary
2 cloves of garlic, crushed
2 Spanish onions, peeled
and chopped
900g (2lb) ripe tomatoes,
roughly chopped
3 tbsp tomato purée
salt and freshly ground
black pepper
pinch of sugar (optional)
two 250g (8.82oz) pkts fresh
tagliatelle verdi
125g (4oz) vegetarian Cheddar or
mature Cheddar cheese, diced
sprigs of fresh rosemary
to garnish

Heat the oil in a large frying pan, add the rosemary, garlic and onions then cook until the onion is golden.

Stir in the tomatoes, tomato purée, a little salt and plenty of freshly ground black pepper. Cover and simmer gently for 10 minutes until the tomatoes cook down to make a rich, thick sauce. Remove the sprig of rosemary, taste and adjust the seasoning; add a pinch of sugar if the flavour is a little acidic.

Meanwhile, cook the fresh pasta in a large pan according to the packet instructions. Drain, return to the pan and add the sauce and the cheese. Toss thoroughly. Garnish with sprigs of rosemary.

Serve with crusty Granary bread and the Leaf and Nut Salad.

LEAF AND NUT SALAD

Rinse and shake dry a selection of salad leaves such as the purple tinged Lollo Rosso and some crisp iceberg leaves. Tear into pieces, then place in a salad bowl with a little vinaigrette dressing of your choice. Toss thoroughly just before serving. Sprinkle with a variety of toasted nuts such as pine nuts, walnuts or almonds, if liked.

PEACHES WITH PASSION FRUIT

Serves 4
60 Calories a portion

4 ripe peaches or nectarines,
peeled if liked
2 passion fruit
fresh mint sprigs, to decorate
Amaretti biscuits, to serve

Put the peaches or nectarines on individual serving dishes with a little of the pulp from the passion fruit and decorate with the mint sprigs. Chill until ready to serve. Accompany with Amaretti biscuits.

Clockwise from top, Peaches with Passion Fruit, Fresh Tagliatelle with Cheese and Tomato Sauce and Leaf and Nut Salad

ON YOUR MARKS. . .

● *Prepare the fruit for the dessert, cover and leave in the fridge until ready to serve*

● *Prepare the ingredients for the sauce then leave to simmer*

● *Meanwhile, put a large pan of water on to boil for the pasta*

● *Rinse and thoroughly dry the salad leaves and place in a salad bowl with the dressing*

● *Cook the pasta according to the packet instructions. Drain*

● *Mix the pasta with the sauce and cheese. Toss the salad and serve immediately*

SPICY VEGETARIAN SUPPER

Here's the perfect quick menu for a tasty vegetarian supper
that meat-eaters will also love

Eggs with Spicy Sauce

Sesame Vegetables

Fresh Mango

EGGS WITH SPICY SAUCE

Serves 4
185 Calories a portion

6 eggs
150g (6oz) low fat soft cheese
½-1 tbsp concentrated curry sauce
or paste
4 tbsp Greek yogurt
few sprigs of fresh coriander, to
garnish
TO SERVE:
4 nan or pitta breads (see
Cook's Note)

Boil the eggs for about 8 minutes, drain, plunge into cold water and leave to cool for a few minutes before peeling off the shells. Halve.

Meanwhile put the soft cheese, curry sauce or paste and yogurt in a small pan and whisk until it starts to boil. Spoon on to 4 warmed dinner plates and place the halved eggs on top. Garnish with the coriander and serve with nan or pitta bread.

COOK'S NOTE
More and more large supermarkets are selling Indian nan breads in their bakery section. Pitta breads are the nearest substitute. Alternatively serve with boiled basmati rice.

SESAME VEGETABLES

Serves 4
235 Calories a portion

25g (1oz) butter
1 tbsp sesame or olive oil
3 tbsp sesame seeds
1 onion, finely chopped
1 red pepper, de-seeded and diced
225g (8oz) potatoes, scrubbed
and diced
225g (8oz) carrots, diced
225g (8oz) turnips or swede, diced
225g (8oz) parsnips, diced
2 tsp paprika
salt and freshly ground
black pepper

Heat the butter and oil in a large frying pan. Add the sesame seeds and cook for 1 minute. Stir in the onion and pepper and fry for 2 minutes. Add the remaining vegetables and seasoning then cook, stirring occasionally until all the vegetables are just soft.

Serve in a hot dish with a little more paprika sprinkled on top if liked.

DESSERT CHOICE

Follow the main meal with wedges of fresh ripe mango, served if you wish with scoops of your favourite sorbet or ice cream.

Eggs with Spicy Sauce, Sesame Vegetables and fresh mango slices to follow

ON YOUR MARKS. . .

● *Put a pan of water on to boil for the eggs*

● *Boil the eggs while preparing and cooking the vegetables*

● *Drain the eggs, set aside. Put the nan or pittas in the oven to warm with the serving plates and dishes*

● *Prepare the fresh mango, cover and put in the fridge to chill*

● *Spoon the vegetables into a serving dish and keep warm in the oven*

● *Make the curry sauce. Serve with shelled, halved hard-boiled eggs and accompany with the nan or pitta breads and the sesame vegetables*

AN ITALIAN-STYLE VEGETARIAN MEAL

An imaginative menu that's ready in moments –
and a perfect choice for non-meat eaters too

Pasta with Creamy Vegetable Medley

Mixed Leaf Salad with Hazelnut Dressing

Baked Figs with Ginger Honey

ON YOUR MARKS. . .

- *Switch the oven on to 180°C (350°F) gas 4*

- *Put the hazelnuts for the salad into the oven to toast*

- *Finely cut the vegetables for the pasta sauce and set aside*

- *Prepare the figs for the dessert, but don't bake yet*

- *Put a pan of salted water on to boil for pasta. Meanwhile soften the vegetables for the sauce in the butter*

- *Wash and prepare the mixed salad leaves*

- *Add the pasta to the boiling water, and cook according to packet instructions*

- *Chop the hazelnuts and mix the dressing ingredients. Toss into the salad leaves*

- *Finish pasta sauce and add to the drained pasta*

- *The figs can be baked in the oven while you're eating the pasta course*

Clockwise from top left, Pasta with Creamy Vegetable Medley, Mixed Leaf Salad with Hazelnut Dressing, and Baked Figs with Ginger Honey

PASTA WITH CREAMY VEGETABLE MEDLEY

Serves 4
460 Calories a portion

350g (12oz) fresh pasta or
225g (8oz) dried
15g (½oz) butter
1 large carrot, peeled and cut into fine matchsticks
1 leek, washed and cut into thin shreds
1 courgette, cut into fine matchsticks
½ small yellow pepper, deseeded and cut into fine strips
150g (5oz) Boursin (herb and garlic soft cheese)
125ml (4fl oz) milk
freshly ground white pepper

Bring a pan of salted water to the boil. Add the pasta and cook for 3-12 minutes according to instructions.

Melt the butter in a pan and add the carrots. Stir to coat in the butter then cover and soften for 1 minute. Stir in the rest of the vegetables and cook for 3-4 minutes until tender. Add the Boursin cheese and milk and heat gently, stirring until the cheese has melted to give a smooth creamy sauce. Season to taste.

Drain the pasta and toss in the sauce. Serve with the salad.

MIXED LEAF SALAD WITH HAZELNUT DRESSING

Serves 4
180 Calories a portion

50g (2oz) skinned hazelnuts
variety of salad leaves
3 tbsp olive oil
1 tbsp red wine vinegar
1 tsp coarse grain mustard
salt and freshly ground black pepper

Place the hazelnuts in a baking tin and toast at the top of the oven at 180°C (350°F) gas 4 for 20-25 minutes until golden. Chop roughly.

Mix together in a salad bowl a selection of salad leaves such as Lollo Rosso, frisée (curly endive), oak leaf and iceberg.

Mix the olive oil with the vinegar, mustard and seasoning. Stir in the hazelnuts and toss onto salad leaves at the last minute.

BAKED FIGS WITH GINGER HONEY

Serves 4
65 Calories a portion

4 fresh figs
15g (½oz) butter
2 tbsp honey with stem ginger (see Cook's Note)
1 tbsp medium sherry
Greek yogurt, to serve (optional)

Cut into the top of each fig 3 times with a sharp knife, to give a star shape, then gently squeeze the figs so they open out like a flower.

Grease an ovenproof dish with the butter. Place the figs in the dish and spoon half a tablespoon of the honey into each fig. Pour over the sherry.

Bake in the oven at 180°C (350°F) gas 4 for 15-20 minutes. Serve hot with Greek yogurt if liked.

COOK'S NOTE
Honey with stem ginger is available ready mixed from many supermarkets. To make your own, blend two tablespoons clear honey with one piece freshly chopped stem ginger. Alternatively use ginger marmalade.

SPEEDY VEGETARIAN SUPPER

Here's a quick meal vegetarians and meat-eaters will love

COURGETTE AND BASIL RISOTTO

Serves 4
430 Calories a portion

2 tbsp olive oil
2 tbsp shelled pistachio nuts, or
peanuts if preferred
125g (4oz) baby button
mushrooms
1 onion, finely chopped
1 clove of garlic, crushed
350g (12oz) arborio (risotto) rice
1.3 litres (2.¼pints) boiling
vegetable stock made with
1 stock cube
1 tbsp white wine vinegar
salt and freshly ground
black pepper
350g (12oz) small courgettes,
sliced
1 tbsp fresh basil, finely shredded

Melt the oil in a large saucepan, add the pistachio nuts and cook for 1 minute to brighten the colour of the nuts. Remove them from the pan with a draining spoon and put aside.

Add the mushrooms and cook over a high heat for 2-3 minutes, stirring until golden. Stir in the onion and garlic and cook for a further minute before stirring in the rice.

Pour over the boiling vegetable stock and wine vinegar. Bring back to the boil, season and simmer for 10 minutes, stirring often. Add the sliced courgettes and cook for 10 minutes more or until all the stock has been absorbed.

Serve immediately, topped with the cooked pistachio nuts and the shredded basil.

GREEN LEAF SALAD

Serves 4
50 Calories a portion

Wash and finely shred 1 small head of Chinese leaves, mix with a large handful of watercress sprigs and scatter over some stoned black olives. Sprinkle over a little orange or grapefruit juice (you could squeeze any fruit left over from preparing the dessert, for example) and a little salad oil (such as sunflower, hazelnut or walnut).

Season just before serving.

CITRUS, HONEY AND ALMOND SALAD

Serves 4
145 Calories a portion

4 oranges
1 pink grapefruit
1 lime, juice only
4 tbsp clear acacia honey
1.½tsp rose-water
125g (4oz) blanched almond
slivers, toasted
dessert biscuits, to serve
(optional)

Cut all the pith and rind from the oranges and grapefruit with a sharp knife. Hold the fruit one at a time over a bowl to catch any juice and cut between the segment membranes to release each segment but not the tough membrane. Mix together the lime juice, honey and rose-water.

Divide the fruit between 4 glasses and spoon the honey mixture over each serving. Sprinkle over the almond slivers. Chill until required. Serve with biscuits if liked.

Courgette and Basil Risotto

Green Leaf Salad

Citrus, Honey and Almond Salad

ON YOUR MARKS. . .

- *Put the water on to boil for the vegetable stock*

- *Start the risotto and leave to simmer*

- *Wash and prepare the Green Leaf Salad and put in the fridge to keep fresh until required*

- *Add the courgettes to the risotto after 10 mins cooking time*

- *Toast almonds for the Citrus, Honey and Almond Salad, while preparing the fruit. Chill in the fridge until ready to eat*

- *Toss the leaf salad in the dressing, and sprinkle the pistachio nuts and basil over the risotto before serving*

Courgette and Basil Risotto, Green Leaf Salad and Citrus, Honey and Almond Salad

QUICK ITALIAN MEAL

For a speedy vegetarian meal from Italy,
try tomato pasta served with a refreshing salad

Pasta Pomodoro

Radicchio and Frisée Salad

Melon and Mango with Cointreau

PASTA POMODORO

Serves 4
300 Calories a portion

**225g (8oz) dried pasta bows
(farfalle)
2 tbsp olive oil
2 cloves garlic, crushed
1 small aubergine, cut into chunks
2 small courgettes, sliced
125g (4oz) baby button
mushrooms, washed
400g (14oz) can chopped
tomatoes
8 black olives, halved and stoned
salt and freshly ground
 black pepper
1 tsp pesto (basil) sauce
fresh basil leaves, to garnish
(optional)
1 loaf of olive or olive oil bread
(see Cook's Note)**

Cook the pasta in a large pan of boiling salted water for 10-12 minutes, or according to packet instructions.

Meanwhile heat the olive oil and add the garlic and aubergine. Cook for 3-4 minutes to soften the aubergine, then add the courgettes and mushrooms. Cook, stirring, for a further 3-4 minutes then add the tomatoes, olives and seasoning. Bring to the boil, simmer for 10 minutes, then stir in the pesto sauce.

Drain the pasta and top with the sauce and basil leaves, if using, before serving.

Serve with olive or olive oil bread.

COOK'S NOTE
Olive bread has whole stoned olives mixed into the dough before baking and olive oil 'ciabatta' bread has just the oil. Both are particularly crusty and delicious if reheated in the oven before serving and are available from most large supermarkets and good delicatessens.

Pasta Pomodoro, Radicchio and Frisée Salad and Melon and Mango with Cointreau

RADICCHIO AND FRISÉE SALAD

Serves 4
65 Calories a portion

**4 large radicchio leaves or 2 heads of red chicory, washed
1 large handful of frisée (curly endive), washed
½ lemon, juice only
2 tbsp olive oil
salt and freshly ground
black pepper**

Tear the salad leaves into bite-sized pieces and place in a large salad bowl. Just before serving the salad squeeze the lemon juice over the leaves and then sprinkle on the olive oil. Season well with salt and plenty of freshly ground black pepper then toss the leaves well until they are lightly and evenly coated in the lemon and oil dressing.

MELON AND MANGO WITH COINTREAU

Serves 4
70 Calories a portion

**1 large orange, juice only
1 lime, grated rind and juice
2 tbsp Cointreau or Grand Marnier
1 small Charentais melon
1 small mango**

Place the orange juice and the lime juice and rind in a small pan and boil for 3 minutes to reduce the sauce by a third. Remove from the heat. Pour in the liqueur and set aside.

Meanwhile, peel the melon and mango, remove the seeds from the melon and the stone from the mango then chop the flesh into large pieces. Place the fruit in a bowl and pour over the warm sauce. Set aside to marinate until ready to serve.

CREATIVE VEGETARIAN MEAL FOR FOUR

Vegetarian cook Sarah Brown puts together a delicious two-course meal for four

Cheese and Leek Ramekins

Hot Marinated Mushrooms

Tomatoes with Green Onions

Spiced Fruit Compote

CHEESE AND LEEK RAMEKINS

A simple savoury bake which cooks quickly in individual ramekins. Fresh breadcrumbs make the texture more substantial, yet the end result is still light. Use a strong cheese.
Serves 4
300 Calories a portion

1 tbsp oil
500g (1lb) leeks, finely sliced
1 clove of garlic, crushed
4 eggs, beaten
50g (2oz) fresh wholemeal
breadcrumbs
125g (4oz) vegetarian Cheddar
cheese, grated
1 tsp dried tarragon
salt and freshly ground
black pepper
butter, for greasing
fresh parsley, to garnish

Heat the oil and gently cook the leeks and garlic for 10 minutes. Mix together the eggs, breadcrumbs, cheese and tarragon. Then add the cooked leeks and season well.

Grease four large (150ml/¼ pint) ramekin dishes with butter. Spoon in the leek mixture and bake at 200°C (400°F) gas 6 for 15 minutes.

Leave to stand for a minute or so, then run a knife round the edge and turn out. Serve immediately, garnished with parsley.

HOT MARINATED MUSHROOMS

You need a succulent side vegetable to complement the texture of the Cheese and Leek Ramekins. This recipe is easy to prepare and is a tasty way of cooking mushrooms.
Serves 4
75 Calories a portion

25g (1oz) butter
375g (12oz) button mushrooms
DRESSING:
1 lemon, 2 tbsp juice and
1 tsp grated rind
1 tsp clear honey
1 tsp prepared mustard
1 tsp dried thyme
salt and freshly ground
black pepper

Gently melt the butter, then add the mushrooms and cook for 5 minutes. Mix the dressing ingredients together. Remove the pan from the heat and pour in the dressing. Serve hot.

Cheese and Leek Ramekins, Hot Marinated Mushrooms and Tomatoes with Green Onions (recipe on page 39)

TIMEPLAN FOR SERVING LUNCH AT 1.00PM

12.30 Set the oven at 200°C (400°F) gas 6. Mix the dried fruit salad with the remaining ingredients and bring to the boil. Slice the leeks and start to cook.
12.35 Turn the fruit compote to simmer. Rinse the mushrooms and halve the tomatoes.
12.40 Prepare the remaining ingredients for the Cheese and Leek Ramekins. Butter the ramekins.
12.45 Complete the ramekins and place in the oven with the flaked almonds.
12.50 Start to cook the mushrooms. Mix the dressing for the mushrooms. Mix the yogurt and honey. Grill the tomatoes.
12.55 Remove the almonds from the oven. Toss the mushrooms in the dressing. Garnish with tomatoes.
1.00 Remove the compote from the heat. Take the ramekins from the oven, turn out and serve with the mushrooms and tomatoes. When ready to serve the pudding, remove the spices and decorate with toasted almonds.

TOMATOES WITH GREEN ONIONS

A quick colourful accompaniment of grilled tomatoes garnished with spring onions.
Serves 4
35 Calories a portion

6-8 tomatoes, halved
a little olive oil
2 spring onions, trimmed and finely chopped
freshly ground black pepper

Brush the tomatoes with a little olive oil. Grill for 5-7 minutes until just tender.
Garnish with spring onions and season with black pepper.

WINE CHOICE
The new wave of dry-ish German wines (labelled halbtrocken or medium dry) are ideal with the first course; look for the grape names Riesling, Silvaner or Müller-Thurgau. Anything from Alsace would make a good alternative, as would beer or lager. The spiced fruit needs more weight, warmth and a little sweetness: a dry to medium Madeira such as Sercial or Verdelho, medium dry amontillado or oloroso sherry, or a chilled ten year old tawny port.

SPICED FRUIT COMPOTE

Dried fruit salad is a useful item to keep in the store cupboard. Stewed with spices and served with a honey-sweetened yogurt it makes an excellent dessert.
Serves 4
285 Calories a portion

250g (8oz) dried fruit salad (see Cook's Note)
600ml (1 pint) apple juice
1 stick cinnamon
1 bay leaf
4 allspice berries
25g (1oz) flaked almonds, to decorate
SAUCE:
225g (8oz) carton Greek yogurt
2-3 tsp clear honey

Mix the fruit salad with the apple juice and spices in a saucepan. Bring the mixture to the boil, then cover and simmer for 25 minutes.
Toast the almonds on a baking sheet at 200°C (400°F) gas 6 for 7-10 minutes or until lightly browned.
For the sauce, mix together the yogurt and honey.
To serve the fruit compote, remove the spices, then spoon the mixture into bowls, decorate with toasted almonds, then hand the yogurt sauce round separately.

COOK'S NOTE
Dried fruit salad usually contains a mixture of apple rings, apricots, prunes, figs and either peaches or pears. It's available from health food stores and larger supermarkets.

Spiced Fruit Compote served with yogurt sauce

EASY VEGETARIAN DINNER

An ideal meal for those occasions when time is limited

TAGLIATELLE WITH COURGETTES AND LEMON CREAM

Fresh pasta is so quick and easy to prepare – it only needs a few minutes cooking so makes an ideal meal when time is short. If you can't buy fresh pasta the dried variety will be equally suitable although it will need to be cooked for a longer time.
Serves 4
455 Calories a portion

375g (12oz) fresh tagliatelle verdi (spinach pasta)
25g (1oz) butter
4 large courgettes, diced
1 lemon, grated rind and juice
salt and freshly ground
black pepper
300ml (½pint) single cream

Cook the pasta in boiling salted water. Meanwhile melt the butter then fry the courgettes and lemon rind until the courgettes have softened. Add a tablespoon of lemon juice and seasoning, and allow to bubble. Carefully add the cream and gently heat through.

Drain the pasta and place on a serving platter or into individual bowls. Spoon over the sauce and serve immediately.

SALAD OF LEAVES

Serves 4
75 Calories a portion

Rinse a selection of different salad leaves such as Webbs lettuce, chicory, oak leaf lettuce and frisée (curly endive). Drain thoroughly then toss in three tablespoons of Italian or French salad dressing.

LIQUEUR STRAWBERRIES

Strawberries soaked in liqueur make a really special dessert.
Serves 4
215 Calories a portion

500g (1lb) small strawberries, rinsed and hulled
3-4 tbsp blackcurrant cordial
1-2 tbsp blackcurrant liqueur (crème de cassis) or gin
fresh mint, to decorate
4-8 shortbread biscuits (petticoat tails), to serve

Mix the strawberries, cordial and liqueur in a glass serving bowl and leave in a cool place until ready to serve. Stir and decorate with mint just before serving.

Place the bowl on a large plate and surround with the shortbread.

Tagliatelle with Courgettes and Lemon Cream

Salad of Leaves

Liqueur Strawberries

TIMEPLAN FOR SERVING DINNER AT 7.30PM

7.00 *Prepare the Liqueur Strawberries, put in a serving bowl and surround with shortbread. Leave in a cool place.*
7.08 *Dice the courgettes and fry in the lemon and butter.*
7.15 *Put a large pan of salted water on to boil. Then start to prepare the leaves for the salad.*
7.20 *Put the pasta on to boil. Complete the salad and toss with the dressing.*
7.25 *Add the cream and plenty of seasoning to the courgettes to make the sauce.*
7.30 *Drain the pasta and spoon over the sauce, serve with the salad and crusty bread.*

A delicious vegetarian meal

AN AMERICAN-STYLE SUMMER LUNCH

A crisp, hearty American-style salad followed by a super-quick dessert using seasonal fruits. Just right for a summer lunch

HOT CHICKEN AND BACON SALAD

A substantial main-meal salad of avocado, tomatoes and crispy lettuce topped with hot chicken, smoked bacon and croûtons. Served with dressing laced with meat juices and accompanied by crusty bread.
Serves 4
435 Calories a portion

1 tbsp oil
3 boneless chicken breasts, cut into strips
4 rashers smoked bacon, cut into strips
½ iceberg lettuce, shredded, or torn into pieces
1 large or 2 small avocados, peeled, stoned and sliced
4 tomatoes, cut into wedges
25g (1oz) garlic croûtons (see Cook's Note)
4 tbsp Italian or French dressing

Heat the oil in a frying pan then cook the chicken and bacon for about 8 minutes, stirring occasionally.

Meanwhile arrange the lettuce, avocado and tomatoes in the base of a large serving bowl.

Add the croûtons to the pan to heat through then remove the chicken, bacon and croûtons with a draining spoon and scatter over the salad ingredients.

Stir the dressing into the pan juices, pour over the salad and serve immediately with hunks of fresh crusty bread.
Not suitable for freezing

BLACKBERRY AND STRAWBERRY SHORTCAKE

This takes less than five minutes to prepare, yet makes a really special dessert. The fruit could be altered to whatever seasonal soft fruits are available, such as raspberries, peaches, fresh apricots, plums or stoned cherries.
Serves 4
255 Calories a portion

one 23cm (7in) round shortbread (petticoat tails)
225g (8oz) carton Greek yogurt
75g (3oz) blackberries, hulled
75g (3oz) strawberries, hulled and sliced

Place the shortbread on a serving plate. Spread the yogurt on top of the shortbread. Arrange the blackberries and strawberry slices on top. Chill until ready to serve.
Not suitable for freezing.

COOK'S NOTE
Garlic croûtons can be bought in small packets in many large supermarkets. They're also easy to make and can be prepared ahead and stored in an airtight container until ready to use.

Dice cubes of bread then fry in oil with several crushed cloves of garlic. Season croûtons with a little salt before serving.

Hot Chicken and Bacon Salad

Crusty Bread

Blackberry and Strawberry Shortcake

ON YOUR MARKS. . .

- *Put the shortbread on a serving plate then top with the Greek yogurt and fruit. Chill until ready to serve*

- *Chop the chicken and bacon then leave to cook*

- *Prepare the salad ingredients*

- *Add the croûtons to the pan to heat through then scatter over the salad*

- *Stir the dressing into the pan juices, heat through and pour over the salad. Serve with crusty bread.*

A stunning summer lunch

A SIMPLE PROVENCE-STYLE SUPPER

A simple French-style meal packed with summer vegetables

PISTOU

This hearty summer soup, originating from Provence in France, is made from a glorious selection of summer vegetables – leeks, courgettes, carrots and French beans. This tasty blend gets added zest from pesto - a sauce made from basil, Parmesan cheese and olive oil. Served with crusty French bread, a platter of cheeses and fresh fruit it makes an ideal meal to enjoy in the garden on a lazy summer day.
Serves 4
235 Calories a portion

1.¼ litres (2 pints) chicken stock
2 carrots, scrubbed and chopped
2 leeks, washed and sliced
2 courgettes, chopped
250g (8oz) French beans, halved
250g (8oz) tomatoes, chopped
1 clove garlic, crushed
50g (2oz) short-cut macaroni
400g (14oz) can cannellini or butter beans, drained
2-3 tbsp pesto sauce (see Cook's Note)
salt and freshly ground black pepper
TO SERVE:
French bread

Put the stock in a pan and bring to the boil. Add the vegetables and garlic then cover and leave to cook for 10 minutes. Stir in the pasta then cook for about 10-15 minutes more until the pasta is cooked but the vegetables are still quite firm.

Add the beans, pesto and seasoning to taste, return to the boil then serve with the crusty bread.

TO FREEZE: cool and pack into a rigid container. Use within 4 months. TO SERVE: thaw completely at room temperature. Reheat gently in a pan. Don't be tempted to reheat the block of soup while still frozen as the pasta will break up.

COOK'S NOTE
Small jars of pesto sauce are available from delicatessens and large supermarkets; it can also be used as a sauce for pasta.

FRENCH CHEESE PLATTER WITH FRUIT

Instead of making a dessert, serve a selection of fruit and French cheeses after the soup.

For a varied selection, try Roulé, a soft, creamy cheese swirled with a blend of herbs and garlic; Chaumes, a medium-textured cheese with a nutty flavour and yellow rind; Chamois D'Or and Henri IV which both look similar to Brie but each has its own distinctive texture and mild, creamy consistency; and Rambol Fourré Aux Noix, a blended cheese spiked with walnuts.

Serve with a variety of summer fruits such as pears, grapes, apples and fresh apricots.

Pistou
(Provençal Vegetable Soup)

Crusty Bread

French Cheese Platter

Fresh Fruit

ON YOUR MARKS...

● *Prepare the vegetables and put on to cook*

● *Add the pasta to the soup*

● *Lay out a selection of fresh fruit and cheeses on serving platters. Cut up the bread and put in a bread basket*

● *Add the beans and pesto to the soup. Return to the boil. Serve*

Pistou followed by French Cheese Platter with Fruit

LIGHT SUMMER MEAL

Not only fast, but colourful – this menu makes the most of soft summer fruits. Raspberries have been mixed with chicken for a main meal salad, with cherries served in buttery croissants for a dreamy dessert

Chicken and Raspberry Salad

Cherry Croissants

ON YOUR MARKS. . .

- *Cook chicken breasts for salad under grill, unless you are using cold roast chicken*

- *Prepare salad leaves*

- *Whisk together ingredients for raspberry dressing*

- *Stone and roughly chop the cherries for the dessert*

- *Split croissants*

- *Remove cooked chicken from grill, skin if liked and slice*

- *Fill croissants and put aside*

- *Complete salad and serve*

COOK'S NOTE
Lollo Rosso is a variety of red lettuce with curly leaves, similar to frisée (curly endive). Radicchio is a round, purple chicory with white veins. It has a slightly bitter flavour which makes a good contrast to lettuce.

CHICKEN AND RASPBERRY SALAD

A pretty combination of cold chicken and mixed salad leaves (see Cook's Note) tossed in a sweet raspberry dressing.
Serves 4
170 Calories a portion

4 Lollo Rosso leaves, torn into pieces
4 frisée (curly endive) leaves, torn into small pieces
¼ small radicchio, thinly shredded
1 small head chicory, shredded
3 boneless chicken breasts, cooked and sliced
RASPBERRY DRESSING:
3 tbsp olive oil
1 tbsp raspberry or white wine vinegar
salt and freshly ground black pepper
75g (3oz) firm raspberries or small strawberries, if preferred
2 tsp demerara sugar

Mix the salad leaves on a serving platter with the chicken pieces.

Whisk the olive oil and the vinegar together and season well. Pour over the salad and toss lightly.

Scatter the raspberries or strawberries over the salad and sprinkle with the sugar.

Serve immediately before the salad leaves become limp and soggy with the dressing.

CHERRY CROISSANTS

Croissants can make a deliciously fast dessert filled with fresh fruit and creamy fromage frais.
Serves 4
270 Calories each

4 croissants
two 45g pots strawberry-flavoured fromage frais
125g (4oz) fresh cherries, stoned and roughly chopped
icing sugar, for dusting
extra cherries and fresh leaves, to decorate (optional)

Split the croissants almost in half. Spread fromage frais on the bottom half of each croissant and spoon chopped cherries on top. Close up and serve dusted with icing sugar. Decorate the plates with extra cherries and fresh leaves, if liked.

Chicken and Raspberry Salad and Cherry Croissants

SUMMERTIME SUPPER

This main meal salad, served with two dressings, is ideal for a summer's day –
when the last thing you want is to slave over a hot stove!
Follow with a scrumptious fruit meringue

Pasta and Pepper Salad

Cherry and Plum Meringue

- *Put a pan of salted water on to boil for the pasta*

- *Heat the grill and char the skin of the red pepper. Place the pepper in a plastic food bag to cool*

- *Put the pasta on to cook*

- *Prepare the other salad ingredients and place in a bowl with the pasta bows once cooked and cooled*

- *Make up the lime and red pepper dressings*

- *Cook the cherries and plums and whisk up the meringue. Spoon the fruit into a flameproof dish and top with meringue. Leave to one side*

- *Toss salad in the lime dressing and serve with crusty bread and the red pepper dressing*

- *Just before serving the dessert, brown the top of the meringue under the grill*

Pasta and Pepper Salad, tossed in one tasty dressing and served with another. Follow with Cherry and Plum Meringue

PASTA AND PEPPER SALAD

Serves 4
380 Calories a portion

SALAD:
175g (6oz) dried pasta bows (farfalle)
1 green pepper
1 yellow pepper
¼ cucumber
75g (3oz) Bavarian smoked cheese or Bruder Basil
4 slices smoked ham
a few fresh coriander leaves
DRESSINGS:
½ small red pepper, deseeded and cut into 4
1 lime, grated rind and juice
2 tbsp olive oil
4 tbsp fresh chopped coriander
2 spring onions
75g (3oz) low-fat cream cheese
salt and freshly ground black pepper
TO SERVE:
crusty bread

Place the pasta bows in a large pan of salted boiling water. Boil for 10 minutes or until tender.

Meanwhile place the red pepper for the dressing under a heated grill to char the skin. Cool in a plastic bag – the steam created helps to loosen the skin. Peel away the skin and discard. Cool the pepper further in cold water if necessary.

Deseed and slice the green and yellow peppers for the salad. Cut the cucumber and cheese into short sticks and the ham into large pieces. Mix all the prepared ingredients together in a bowl. Drain the cooked pasta bows and cool under cold running water. Drain well and add to the bowl with the coriander leaves.

Mix together the lime rind and juice with the olive oil and 2 tablespoons of the chopped coriander, then toss into the salad. Place the cooled, skinned red pepper in a blender or food processor with the spring onions, cream cheese,

remaining chopped coriander and seasoning. Blend until smooth. Serve with the salad and accompany with the crusty bread.

VEGETARIAN NOTE
Omit the ham and choose a cheese without animal rennet, such as a vegetarian Cheddar or feta cheese.

CHERRY AND PLUM MERINGUE

Serves 4
160 Calories a portion

7g (¼ oz) butter
225g (8oz) sweet cherries, stoned
225g (8oz) dessert plums, stoned
1 small orange, grated rind and juice
2 egg whites
125g (4oz) caster sugar

Melt the butter in a frying pan and add the pitted cherries and stoned plums. Cook for 2 minutes, stirring continuously, then add the rind and juice of the orange. Allow to bubble and reduce until only a little juice is left in the pan. Spoon the fruit into a flameproof dish and set aside.

Whisk the egg whites until stiff (preferably with an electric beater), then gradually whisk in the caster sugar until the egg whites are stiff and shiny. Spread the meringue over the fruit and place under a low heated grill for 2-3 minutes or until the meringue starts to turn golden.

A RELAXED
SUMMER LUNCH

Ready in moments, this is the perfect choice for a relaxed lunch. Spicy chicken and
fresh seasonal vegetables followed by a luscious strawberry dessert

Sesame Spiced Chicken

Avocado, Watercress and Tomato Salad

Peppered New Potatoes

Strawberries Cassis

SESAME SPICED CHICKEN

Serves 4
245 Calories a portion

4 boneless chicken breasts, skinned
1 egg, beaten
4 tbsp sesame seeds
1 tsp each ground coriander and cumin
salt and freshly ground black pepper
25g (1oz) butter
1 tbsp olive oil
watercress, to garnish (optional)

Carefully coat the chicken breasts first in the beaten egg and then in the sesame seeds, coriander and cumin and seasoning.

Heat the butter and oil in a non-stick frying pan and when bubbling add the chicken.

Cook for about 5 minutes each side, depending on the thickness of the chicken breasts, until the outside is golden and the chicken is cooked all the way through. Slice the chicken breasts and fan out attractively.

Serve with the salad and new potatoes and garnish with watercress, if liked.
Not suitable for freezing.

AVOCADO, WATERCRESS AND TOMATO SALAD

Peel, halve, stone and slice a ripe avocado into a salad bowl then toss in a few tablespoons of vinaigrette or Italian dressing, and some freshly ground black pepper. Add a large handful of washed watercress sprigs and 3 sliced tomatoes. Toss together and serve immediately.

PEPPERED NEW POTATOES

Boil 450g (1lb) small new potatoes, still in their skins, for 8-10 minutes, depending on their size. Drain then toss with a generous knob of ready-made black pepper butter (or butter with plenty of freshly milled black pepper). Serve immediately.

STRAWBERRIES CASSIS

Makes 4
130 Calories each

450g (1lb) ripe strawberries, rinsed if necessary
4 tbsp reduced-sugar blackcurrant cordial or crème de cassis
four 45g (1.¾oz) pots strawberry fromage frais (see Cook's Note)

Reserve 2 large strawberries for decoration then hull and slice the remainder into a bowl. Add the blackcurrant cordial or crème de cassis, stir until the strawberries are well coated. Divide between 4 individual sundae dishes.

Spoon the strawberry fromage frais on top. Halve the reserved strawberries then use to decorate the desserts. Leave the deserts in a cool place, but don't refrigerate as the delicate flavour of the strawberries will be impaired.
Not suitable for freezing.

COOK'S NOTE
Strawberry fromage frais is a sweetened and flavoured low-fat soft cheese. It's delicious on its own or combined with fruit.

ON YOUR MARKS. . .

- *Make the strawberry dessert, then leave in a cool place until ready to serve*

- *Coat the chicken breasts in the egg, sesame seeds and spices*

- *Scrub the new potatoes then put a pan of lightly salted water on to boil*

- *Start to cook the chicken. Add the potatoes to the boiling water, cover and leave to boil*

- *Make the salad, keeping an eye on the chicken and turning the pieces over occasionally*

- *Slice the chicken and serve with the potatoes and salad*

A scrumptious light lunch – enjoy with a chilled glass of white wine

OUTDOOR SUMMER SUPPER

Here's a light, refreshing meal for four -
very easy to make and great for outdoor summer eating

Summer Niçoise

Fresh Baked Garlic Rolls

*Strawberry
Caramel Cream*

SUMMER NIÇOISE

Serves 4
290 Calories a portion

3 eggs
125g (4oz) French beans, trimmed
**200g (7oz) pkt ready washed
iceberg lettuce**
**200g (7oz) can tuna in brine,
drained**
**50g (1.76oz) can anchovy fillets,
drained**
12 black olives, stoned
3 tomatoes
**400g (14oz) can artichoke hearts,
drained**
DRESSING:
6 tbsp sunflower oil
2 tbsp lemon juice
1 tbsp Dijon mustard
**salt and freshly ground
black pepper**
2 tbsp freshly chopped parsley
1 clove garlic (optional)

Put the eggs in a saucepan of cold
water. Bring to the boil and cook for
8 minutes.

Meanwhile, cut beans into 2.5cm
(1in) lengths and cook in boiling
water for 3 minutes. Drain, cool
quickly in cold water then drain again.
Tear the lettuce into bite-sized pieces
and put into a salad bowl with the
beans. Flake the tuna into large
pieces and add to the bowl with the
anchovy fillets and olives.

Drain the eggs, crack their shells
and cool them quickly under running
cold water (to prevent discolouring
and ease peeling). Drain and peel the
eggs and then cut them and the
tomatoes into quarters. Cut the arti-
chokes in half, and add to the salad
bowl with the eggs and tomatoes.

Mix all the dressing ingredients
together and pour over the salad.
Toss together gently and serve with
the freshly baked rolls.

FRESH BAKED
GARLIC ROLLS

Serves 4
145 Calories each

Heat oven to 220°C (425°F) gas 7.
Place a sliver of herb and garlic butter
on top of 4 part-baked bread rolls.
Cook on a baking sheet for 8-10 minutes until crisp and golden.

STRAWBERRY
CARAMEL CREAM

Serves 4
240 Calories a portion

4 tbsp demerara sugar
225g (8oz) fresh strawberries
**½ tsp orange flower water or the
grated rind of 1 small orange**
150ml (¼pint) double cream
225g (8oz) Greek yogurt
2 tbsp icing sugar
**extra strawberries and strawberry
leaves, to decorate**

Draw or mark a circle on a large
sheet of foil set on a baking sheet,
using a 575ml (1pint) soufflé dish as
a guide. Brush the foil lightly with oil.
Preheat the grill.

Sprinkle the demerara sugar in an
even layer, about 1cm (½in) in from
the edge of the circle. Place under
the grill until the sugar is bubbling
and just beginning to caramelise.
Mark the circle into quarters with a
damp, sharp knife and leave to cool
and harden.

Hull and halve the strawberries
and place in the soufflé dish. Sprinkle
a few drops of orange flower water
or the grated orange rind over them.
Whip the cream until soft peaks
form. Fold in the yogurt and icing
sugar. Spoon over the strawberries
and smooth the surface.

Carefully peel the foil from the
cooled caramelised pieces and place
on top of the dish just before serving.
Decorate with the extra strawberries
and the strawberry leaves.

Summer Niçoise and Stawberry
Caramel Cream

ON YOUR MARKS. . .

- Turn on the grill and set the oven to 220°C (425°F) gas 7

- Make the caramel for the dessert and set aside to cool and harden

- Put the eggs on to hard boil and the beans on to cook while preparing the rest of the salad

- Bake the bread rolls 10 minutes before you are ready to eat

- Finish making the dessert and top with the caramel

A LOW-CALORIE LUNCH FOR FOUR

A tempting menu under 500 Calories a portion, for two courses!

Haddock Julienne

Orange and Coriander Rice

Apricot and Almond Ambrosia

Haddock Julienne with Orange and Coriander Rice

TIMEPLAN FOR SERVING LUNCH AT 1.00PM

12.30 *Set the oven temperature at 190°C (375°F) gas 5. Prepare the fish parcels and set on a baking sheet.*

12.40 *Place the fish parcels in the oven to cook. Prepare the rice and leave to simmer.*

12.45 *Place almonds in a tin and put in oven on top shelf. Remove when golden in about 5 minutes.*

12.50 *Prepare the dessert and place in the fridge to chill. Leave the almonds to cool.*

1.00 *Remove the fish parcels from the oven and serve in the foil with its juices. Serve the rice on a warmed platter.*
When ready to serve the dessert, sprinkle each glass with a few toasted almonds.

HADDOCK JULIENNE

Fresh fish cooked in a foil parcel with strips of colourful vegetables cooks quickly and all the juices and flavours are locked in.
Serves 4
140 Calories a portion

750g (1.½lb) fresh haddock fillet
1 carrot, cut into fine strips
½ leek, trimmed and shredded
150ml (¼ pint) tomato juice
1 tbsp light soy sauce
1 lemon, finely grated rind only
1 tsp chopped fresh dill
8 fresh mint sprigs
salt and freshly ground
black pepper

Cut the fish into 4 neat pieces and place each on a square of foil. Divide the carrot and leek into 4 and scatter them over the fish.

Blend together the tomato juice and soy sauce then pour over the fish. Scatter the lemon rind and dill over the top and add a mint sprig to each parcel. Season to taste.

Bring the foil up round each piece of fish and pleat the edges together on top to make neat parcels. Place on a baking sheet and bake at 190°C (375°F) gas 5 for 20 minutes. Just before serving, neatly unfold the foil, remove the mint sprigs and replace with fresh ones.

ORANGE AND CORIANDER RICE

Rice is an ideal accompaniment for speedy cooking. Here it's cooked in orange juice and flavoured with crushed coriander seeds – don't use ground coriander. Saffron gives the dish a subtle flavour and delightful colour; turmeric, a cheaper substitute, will give a stronger, spicy flavour and a darker colour.
Serves 4
170 Calories a portion

175g (6oz) long grain rice
200ml (7fl oz) orange juice
300ml (½ pint) chicken stock
2 tsp coriander seeds, crushed
(see Cook's Note)
pinch of powdered saffron or
turmeric
pinch of salt

Rinse rice in a sieve under cold running water until the water runs clear. This removes excess starch and prevents the rice turning sticky.

Place the orange juice and chicken stock in a large saucepan and bring to the boil. Stir in the rice, crushed coriander seeds and saffron or turmeric. Season with salt, return to the boil, then reduce the heat to a steady simmer.

Cover the pan and cook for about 15 minutes, until tender. The rice should absorb all the liquid but, if necessary, add a little more stock or orange juice.

COOK'S NOTE
To crush coriander seeds, either use a pestle and mortar or the end of a rolling pin in a bowl. Alternatively, crush the coriander seeds in an electric coffee grinder.

APRICOT AND ALMOND AMBROSIA

Fruit canned in natural juice is a real boon to slimmers as it saves calories as well as tasting really fruity. Use it to make a quick fool with very low-fat fromage frais, for a creamy texture.
Serves 4
150 Calories a portion

two 285g (10oz) cans apricots in
natural juice
1-2 tbsp Amaretto liqueur (see
Cook's Note)
250g (8oz) fromage frais or
Greek yogurt
1 tbsp caster sugar (optional)
1 tbsp flaked almonds, toasted

The finale: Apricot and Almond Ambrosia

Place one can of apricots with the juice in a blender or food processor and purée until smooth. Spoon into 4 dessert glasses. Drain the second can of apricots and purée the fruit only. (The drained juice can be diluted with soda water or sparkling mineral water, for a refreshing drink.) Stir the liqueur and the fromage frais or yogurt into the purée. Sweeten if liked. Spoon into glasses and chill until served.

Sprinkle the dessert with toasted flaked almonds to decorate, just before serving.

COOK'S NOTE
Amaretto is an Italian liqueur with a flavour like ratafia biscuits. An alternative would be a good brandy with a few drops of almond essence.

WINE CHOICE
If you're watching calories, but still like a glass of wine, a spritzer (half wine and half sparkling mineral water) is the ideal compromise at about 40 Calories a glass. It can be made with any light dry white wine, but don't choose anything expensive – it would be sacrilege to dilute it!

DELICIOUS SUMMER DINNER

A quick, colourful summer dinner for four

Barbecued Lamb and Pepper Kebabs

Tabbouleh

Lemon and Hazelnut Ice with Honey

TIMEPLAN FOR SERVING DINNER AT 7.30PM

7.00 *Preheat grill. Pour boiling water on to the bulgar wheat and leave to soak.*
7.03 *Grill hazelnuts then chop.*
7.08 *Cube the lamb and coat in the hoisin sauce. Deseed and chop both the peppers. Thread on to skewers.*
7.20 *Put the kebabs under the grill. Meanwhile, chop the parsley and mint, squeeze the lemon and place in a salad bowl with the olive oil and plenty of seasoning.*
7.25 *Drain the bulgar wheat and squeeze out the excess moisture. Toss with the herbs, lemon and olive oil.*
7.30 *Place on a warmed platter and arrange the kebabs on top. When you are ready to eat the dessert, place scoops of ice creams into sundae dishes, spoon over some honey and sprinkle with the nuts.*

Barbecued Lamb and Pepper Kebabs served with Tabbouleh, followed by Lemon and Hazelnut Ice with Honey

BARBECUED LAMB AND PEPPER KEBABS

Kebabs don't take long to grill and make a colourful main meal. Use lean lamb fillet for a really tender result with very little waste.
Serves 4
450 Calories a portion

750g (1.½lb) lean lamb fillet
6 tbsp hoisin sauce (Chinese barbecue sauce)
1 red pepper
1 yellow pepper

Cut the lamb into cubes and coat in the hoisin sauce.

Deseed the peppers then cut into chunks. Thread on skewers with the meat then grill for about 8-10 minutes turning frequently.

TABBOULEH

This is a salad made from bulgar wheat, a grain which is available from health food shops and some supermarkets. To prepare, soak in boiling water for about 15 minutes then drain and mix with other ingredients. Pre-boiled rice could be used as an alternative, but only use the juice from half a lemon.
Serves 4
160 Calories a portion

Pour boiling water over 12 heaped tablespoons of bulgar wheat in a bowl and leave for 15-20 minutes.

Meanwhile, place the juice from a large lemon in a salad bowl together with 1 tablespoon of olive oil, 12 tablespoons of chopped parsley, 3 tablespoons of chopped mint and one finely chopped onion.

Drain the bulgar wheat in a fine mesh sieve pressing out all the excess water. Add to the salad bowl with plenty of salt and freshly ground black pepper then serve while still warm.

LEMON AND HAZELNUT ICE WITH HONEY

Ice cream and sorbets are delicious served together.
Serves 4
315 Calories a portion

4 scoops of lemon sorbet
4 scoops of vanilla ice cream
4 scoops of hazelnut ice cream
4 tsp clear honey
25g (1oz) toasted hazelnuts, chopped

Pile a scoop of each flavoured ice into a sundae glass then drizzle over the honey and scatter with nuts.

SPECIAL FRIDAY SUPPER

Fancy something different to start the weekend? Try our stylish and unusual Special Friday Supper

SPECIAL SAFFRON AND SEAFOOD RICE

Serves 4
445 Calories a portion

**pinch of saffron strands
575ml (1 pint) boiling water
2 tbsp olive oil
1 onion, chopped
275g (10oz) basmati rice
2 cloves garlic, crushed
1 lemon, grated rind and juice
salt and freshly ground
black pepper
275g (10oz) boneless, skinned
haddock fillets
275g (10oz) pack chilled seafood
cocktail (a mixture of mussels,
squid, cockles and prawns)
8 large chilled, peeled prawns
1 green pepper, deseeded
and chopped
lemon wedges, to serve**

Crush the saffron strands with your fingertips and add to the boiling water. Allow to soak while you are preparing the dish.

Heat the oil in a large frying pan. Add the chopped onion and fry for 5 minutes until beginning to soften but not brown. Add the rice and garlic and cook for 2 minutes, stirring well, until the rice is coated in the oil.

Pour the saffron mixture over the rice and add the lemon rind and juice, salt and plenty of freshly ground black pepper. Bring to the boil, cover and cook for three minutes.

Add the haddock fillets and reduce the heat to a simmer. Cover the pan and cook for four minutes. Add the seafood cocktail, peeled prawns and the chopped green pepper. Cook uncovered for a further 4-5 minutes or until haddock flakes easily, the rice is tender and nearly all the water has been absorbed.

Break the haddock into large pieces and stir lightly to mix all the ingredients together. Serve garnished with lemon wedges to squeeze over the rice.

ICEBERG SALAD WITH HOT WALNUT DRESSING

Serves 4
265 Calories a portion

**50g (2oz) walnut pieces
200g (7oz) packet ready washed
iceberg lettuce
4 tbsp olive oil
1 tbsp white wine vinegar
¾ tsp Dijon mustard
¾ tsp clear honey
salt and freshly ground
black pepper**

Preheat the grill. Put the walnuts on to a baking sheet and grill for 2-3 minutes until lightly toasted. Break the lettuce into bite-sized pieces and place in a salad bowl.

Whisk the oil, vinegar, mustard, honey and seasoning together in a small bowl using a fork. At the last minute add the hot walnuts to the dressing and mix together. Pour over the salad just before serving.

RHUBARB AND GINGER FOOL

Serves 4
150 Calories a portion

**225g (8oz) ready trimmed rhubarb
2 pieces stem ginger, drained
225g (8oz) Greek yogurt with
cream
3 tbsp clear honey
1 tsp demerara sugar**

Wash and drain the rhubarb. Thinly slice and put into a saucepan with 1 tbsp water. Cover and cook for 10 minutes until soft. Spoon into a shallow dish and leave to cool while you finish off the recipe.

Meanwhile, reserve 4 slices of the stem ginger for the decoration, finely chop the rest and put into a bowl with the yogurt and honey. Mix

together and set aside.

Reserve a little cooled rhubarb and fold the rest into the yogurt mixture. Spoon into tall glasses. Decorate with the reserved rhubarb and stem ginger and sprinkle with a little demerara sugar.

Special Saffron and Seafood Rice

Iceberg Salad with Hot Walnut Dressing

Rhubarb and Ginger Fool

ON YOUR MARKS...

- *Put the saffron strands in the boiling water*
- *Cook the rhubarb*
- *Start to cook the special rice. Meanwhile mix together the remaining fool ingredients and set aside*
- *Grill the walnuts and make the salad and dressing*
- *Fold the cooled rhubarb into the fool mixture, spoon into glasses and decorate just before serving*

Special Saffron and Seafood Rice, Iceberg Salad with Hot Walnut Dressing and Rhubarb and Ginger Fool

TASTY MID-WEEK SUPPER

Transform simple lamb chops with this spiced tomato sauce

Lamb with Tomatoes

Spiced Potatoes with Chives

Hot Courgette Salad

Apricot and Cardamom Compote

Lamb with Tomatoes, Hot Courgette Salad, Spiced Potatoes with Chives and Apricot and Cardamom Compote to follow

ON YOUR MARKS. . .

● Cook apricots and set aside when ready

● Meanwhile fry chops then add onion and garlic

● Put water on to boil for the potatoes in a large pan

● Add tomatoes and remaining ingredients to lamb chops

● Cook potatoes

● Steam courgettes over potatoes for the last 8 minutes. Make the lemon dressing

● Finish potatoes

● Toss courgettes in dressing and serve the meal

LAMB WITH TOMATOES

Serves 4
170 Calories a portion

2 tbsp sunflower oil
4 lamb chump chops, trimmed
1 onion, thinly sliced
1 clove garlic, crushed
397g (14oz) can chopped tomatoes
2 tbsp demerara sugar
1 cinnamon stick, broken in two
¼ tsp grated nutmeg
½ tsp dried chilli flakes
salt and freshly ground black pepper
flat leaf parsley, to garnish

Heat the oil in a large frying pan, add chops and cook for 5 minutes, turning once until browned.

Add onion and garlic and cook for a few minutes more until softened. Pour over the tomatoes then add the sugar, cinnamon, nutmeg, chilli flakes and seasoning.

Bring to the boil then simmer for 15 minutes, stirring occasionally, or until the chops are tender.

Serve each portion garnished with a sprig of parsley.

SPICED POTATOES WITH CHIVES

Serves 4
200 Calories a portion

550g (1.¼ lb) new potatoes, scrubbed
salt
25g (1oz) butter
2 tbsp freshly chopped chives
¼ tsp dried chilli flakes

Halve any large potatoes and cook in a large pan of boiling, lightly salted water for 12-15 minutes or until tender. (Choose a large pan so the courgettes can steam above them.) Drain potatoes. Heat the butter in the drained pan. Add the potatoes, chives and chilli flakes and toss together well.

HOT COURGETTE SALAD

Serves 4
70 Calories a portion

350g (12oz) courgettes
½ lemon, grated rind and 2 tbsp juice
2 tbsp sunflower oil
salt and freshly ground black pepper

Trim courgettes and cut into thick diagonal slices. Put into a steamer or colander set over the saucepan with the potatoes, cover and steam for 8 minutes or until tender.

Meanwhile mix the lemon rind and juice, oil and seasoning in a serving dish and toss the courgettes in the dressing.

APRICOT AND CARDAMOM COMPOTE

Serves 4
135 Calories a portion

250g (9oz) pkt ready-to-eat dried apricots
300ml (½ pint) apple juice
1 tbsp clear honey
8 cardamom pods

Put the apricots, apple juice and honey into a saucepan. Crush 4 of the cardamom pods and add to the apricots. Bring to the boil, then reduce heat and simmer for 10 minutes or until tender. Decorate with the reserved cardamoms. Serve with Greek yogurt or ice cream.

SIMPLE OVEN-BAKED SUPPER

This meal is all baked in the oven: a smoky fish dish with spinach and cheese, sesame potatoes and herb baked tomatoes, followed by crunchy syrup tartlets

Haddock Florentine

Thyme Baked Tomatoes

Parmentier Potatoes

Crunchy Syrup Tartlets

HADDOCK FLORENTINE

Serves 4
305 Calories a portion

675g (1.¼lb) smoked haddock
fillets, thawed if frozen, skinned
25g (1oz) butter
freshly ground black pepper
1 tsp ground or freshly grated
nutmeg
4 celery sticks, finely sliced
4 spring onions, trimmed
and sliced
450g (1lb) frozen leaf spinach,
thawed and well drained
(see Cook's Note)
125g (4oz) Red Leicester cheese,
grated

Cut the fish into 10cm (4in) pieces and arrange in a lightly buttered shallow ovenproof dish. Dot with butter and sprinkle with pepper, nutmeg, celery and spring onion. Layer the spinach on top, cover the dish with foil and bake at 220°C (425°F) gas 7 for 10 minutes.

Remove the foil, sprinkle the cheese on top leaving a border of spinach and bake for 10-15 minutes more to melt the cheese.

COOK'S NOTE
Look out for 'free flow' frozen spinach which can be cooked from frozen. To defrost a block of spinach quickly, thaw in the microwave or pour boiling water over, before draining thoroughly.

THYME BAKED TOMATOES

Serves 4
20 Calories a portion

Halve 4 tomatoes and place in a shallow ovenproof dish. Brush with a little oil, sprinkle with fresh or dried thyme and season well. Bake at 220°C (425°F) gas 7 for 10 minutes.

PARMENTIER POTATOES

Serves 4
250 Calories a portion

Cut about 750g (1.½ lb) potatoes into 1cm (½in) dice. Parboil for 5 minutes, drain and toss in a roasting tin in which 25g (1oz) butter has been melted in 2 tablespoons oil. Sprinkle the potatoes with sesame seeds and bake at 220°C (425°F) gas 7 for 20-25 minutes until the potatoes are crisp and golden.

CRUNCHY SYRUP TARTLETS

Makes 8
125 Calories each

8 slices white bread
50g (2oz) butter, melted
2 tbsp golden syrup
50g (2oz) plain or crunchy
nut cornflakes
single cream to serve

Flatten the bread with a rolling pin then stamp out a circle from each slice using a 7.5cm (3in) cutter. Brush one side of each circle with melted butter, press into bun tins and then brush the insides with more melted butter.

Warm the syrup (in the pan used to melt the butter).
Add the cornflakes to the pan, lightly crushing them with your hands. Stir well and spoon the mixture into the prepared bread cases.

Bake at 220°C (425°F) gas 7 for about 10 minutes until crispy and golden. Leave to cool before serving with single cream.

ON YOUR MARKS...

- *Switch the oven on to 220°C (425°F) gas 7*

- *Prepare and parboil the diced potatoes then put them in the oven to roast*

- *Make and put the Haddock Florentine in to cook. Prepare the tomatoes and set aside.*

- *Make and bake the Crunchy Syrup Tartlets*

- *Sprinkle the cheese on the Haddock Florentine and return to the oven with the tomatoes*

- *Serve the potatoes and tomatoes with the fish while the tartlets are cooling*

Haddock Florentine, Parmentier Potatoes, Thyme Baked Tomatoes and Crunchy Syrup Tartlets

HEARTY FAMILY SUPPER

Looking for an easy yet delicious family supper?
Try sausage hotpot, mash and French beans – it's hearty and wholesome

Somerset Sausage Hotpot

Cheese Mash

Herby French Beans

ON YOUR MARKS. . .

- *Prepare the potatoes and put them on to cook*

- *Brown the sausages while preparing the vegetables for the hotpot. Soften the vegetables in the remaining oil, finish off the recipe, cover and leave to cook*

- *Put a pan of water on for the beans. Trim them if using fresh beans and cook them when the water has boiled*

- *Drain and mash the potatoes with the seasoning and stir in the cheese. Pile them into a flameproof dish and place under the grill to brown*

- *Cook the garlic for the beans, then toss in the cooked beans*

- *Serve yogurt and fresh fruit for dessert*

Somerset Sausage Hotpot, Cheese Mash and Herby French Beans

SOMERSET SAUSAGE HOTPOT

Serves 4
330 Calories a portion

450g (1lb) lean pork sausages (see Cook's Note)
2 tbsp oil
2 onions, chopped
2 carrots, peeled and sliced
1 tbsp plain flour
1 sprig of fresh sage or 1 tsp dried
1 sprig fresh thyme or ½ tsp dried
227g (8oz) can chopped tomatoes
1 tbsp tomato purée
300ml (½pint) dry cider
salt and ground black pepper

Brown the sausages in 1 tablespoon of the oil in a frying pan.

Meanwhile heat the remaining oil in a large saucepan and add the onions and carrots. Cook for 5 minutes, stirring occasionally until the onions have softened, then stir in the flour. Add the remaining ingredients and bring to the boil.

Add the sausages then cover and simmer for 15-20 minutes.

COOK'S NOTE
Lean or low-fat sausages are ideal to use in casseroles, hotpots, or other moist methods of cooking. The high meat content means the sausages will firm up rather than falling apart during cooking.

CHEESE MASH

Serves 4
270 Calories a portion

575g (1.¼lb) potatoes, peeled and cut into small pieces
salt and freshly ground black pepper
25g (1oz) butter
1 tbsp milk
pinch of grated nutmeg
75g (3oz) sage Derby cheese, crumbled (see Cook's Note)

Cook the potatoes in boiling salted water for 15-20 minutes or until tender. Drain well and mash the potatoes with the butter, milk, ground pepper and nutmeg until they are quite smooth.

Reserve a little of the cheese for the top and stir in the rest. Pile the mixture into a flameproof serving dish and scatter over the remaining crumbled cheese.

Place the dish under a hot grill until the cheese has melted and is golden on top.

COOK'S NOTE
Sage Derby is a delicious cheese which is delicately marbled with chopped sage. It gives a wonderful flavour to this potato mash.

HERBY FRENCH BEANS

Serves 4
50 Calories a portion

450g (1lb) fresh trimmed or frozen French beans
salt and ground black pepper
1 tbsp walnut or olive oil
1 clove of garlic, sliced thinly
1 tbsp fresh chopped parsley

Cook the beans in a pan of boiling salted water for 5-6 minutes, or until they are just tender.

Heat the oil in a frying pan and cook the sliced garlic until it begins to colour.

Add the drained beans and cook, stirring, for a further 1-2 minutes. Toss in the parsley and pepper just before serving.

A QUICK TASTY SUPPER

A tasty Italian-style risotto served with a hot savoury bread and salad –
just right for when time is short

Tomato and Tuna Risotto

Hot Pesto Bread

Mixed Leaf Salad

TOMATO AND TUNA RISOTTO

Serves 4
245 Calories a portion

25g (1oz) butter
2 large onions, chopped
225g (8oz) long grain rice
2 x 400g (14oz) cans chopped
tomatoes
8 black olives
1 green pepper, deseeded and
chopped
1-2 tbsp pesto sauce
salt and freshly ground
black pepper
213g (7.½ oz) can tuna fish chunks,
drained

Melt the butter in a large frying pan,
add the onions and fry until they
begin to soften. Stir in the rice, toss
around the pan to coat the grains in
the butter then mix in the tomatoes,
olives, green pepper and pesto.
Season to taste, then cover and simmer for 15 minutes.

Gently stir in the tuna, and a little
water if all of the tomato juice has
been absorbed into the rice, then
simmer gently for 5-10 minutes
more until the rice is tender.

Serve immediately.
Not suitable for freezing.

HOT PESTO BREAD

Serves 4-6
300-200 Calories a portion

2-3 tbsp pesto sauce
40g (1.½ oz) butter
1 sesame seed loaf

Beat the pesto sauce into the butter.
Make cuts all along the loaf of bread,
not quite cutting down to the base,
then spread each slice with the
pesto and butter mixture.

Press back into the loaf shape,
wrap in foil then bake at 200°C
(400°F) gas 6 for 20 minutes.

Serve hot with the Tomato and
Tuna Risotto.
TO FREEZE: freeze before baking
and use within 1 month.
TO SERVE: bake the bread from
frozen at the temperature above for
30-35 minutes.

MIXED LEAF SALAD

As the risotto and pesto bread are so
highly seasoned, choose a simple
salad consisting of just a few different leaves and a vinaigrette dressing.
A crisp, juicy iceberg lettuce with the
bitter flavour of endive makes a good
combination. Add the dressing just
before serving.

DESSERT IDEA

For a dessert idea serve slices of
shop-bought cassata – an elaborate,
multi-flavoured Italian ice cream stud-
ded with delicious dried and
candied fruit.

ON YOUR MARKS. . .

- *Set the oven to 200°C (400°F) gas 6*

- *Prepare the ingredients for the risotto, then put the onions on to cook*

- *Make the pesto butter*

- *Add the rice, tomatoes, pepper, seasoning and pesto sauce to the onions, cover and leave to cook*

- *Complete the pesto bread and bake in the oven*

- *Make the salad*

- *Complete the tuna risotto*

- *Serve*

Tomato and Tuna Risotto
served with Hot Pesto Bread
and Mixed Leaf Salad

TURKEY FEAST SUPPER

Transform turkey leftovers into a feast with this special menu for four

Vegetable and Turkey Fricassée

Parmesan Potatoes

Clementine Brûlée

VEGETABLE AND TURKEY FRICASSÉE

Serves 4
285 Calories a portion

25g (1oz) butter
125g (4oz) button mushrooms
2 medium carrots, cut into sticks
2 celery stalks, thinly sliced
1 small onion, cut into wedges
350g (12oz) cooked turkey pieces
150ml (¼pint) dry white wine
50ml (2fl oz) chicken or
turkey stock
2 tsp freshly chopped rosemary or
1 tsp dried
salt and freshly ground
black pepper
2 egg yolks
6 tbsp crème fraîche or
soured cream
1 tbsp fresh chopped parsley

Melt the butter and cook the mushrooms in it until golden. Add the rest of the vegetables and cook for 10 minutes, stirring occasionally until they soften.

Stir in the turkey, wine, stock, rosemary and seasoning. Cover and cook for 5-10 minutes to heat the turkey through.

Mix together the yolks and crème fraîche (or cream) and stir into the pan. Heat gently, stirring all the time until stock thickens, but do not boil. Stir in the chopped parsley and serve immediately.

PARMESAN POTATOES

Serves 4
220-250 Calories a portion

2 tbsp olive oil
575-675g (1.¼lb-1.½lb) large
potatoes, peeled and cut into
large pieces
salt and freshly ground
black pepper
1 tbsp freshly grated Parmesan
cheese

Heat the oil in a frying pan. Add the potatoes and stir well to coat in oil. Reduce heat slightly and cook for 10-15 min or until the potatoes are golden. Sprinkle over seasoning and Parmesan just before serving.

CLEMENTINE BRÛLÉE

Serves 4
160 Calories a portion

12 clementines or mandarins
15g (½oz) butter
3 tbsp vodka
3 tbsp dark brown sugar

Peel 2 of the clementines and cut the rind into fine shreds. Peel the remaining fruit.

Heat the butter and vodka with 2 tbsp of the sugar in a large pan. Add the whole fruit and the fine shreds of peel, cover and cook for 2-3 minutes.

Pour the fruit and juices into a flameproof dish and top with the remaining sugar. Place under a low-heat grill until the sugar just starts to caramelise, then serve.

ON YOUR MARKS...

● Prepare and cook the clementines, transfer to a flameproof dish, sprinkle over the sugar and set aside to finish cooking later

● Peel and cut up the potatoes. Set aside

● Cut up the vegetables and meat and cook the turkey fricassée

● Put the potatoes into the hot oil to cook. Keep an eye on them and stir occasionally

● Stir the egg yolk and cream mixture into the fricassée just before serving

● When the potatoes are golden, drain on absorbent kitchen paper, season and sprinkle over the Parmesan cheese

● Put the oranges under a low-heat grill just before you are ready to eat them

Complement creamy turkey with a light and tangy citrus clementine dessert

MONDAY SUPPER

Turn leftovers from the Sunday roast into a tasty family supper –
and to follow, a nutty plum crumble

Hash Browns

Garlic Grilled Tomatoes

Plum and Almond Crumble

HASH BROWNS

Serves 4
330 Calories a portion

**550g (1.¼lb) new potatoes,
scrubbed (See Cook's Note)
2 tbsp oil
1 large onion, finely chopped
25g (1oz) butter
150g (6oz) cabbage, finely
shredded
175-225g (6-8oz) cooked lamb or
beef, chopped
2 tsp caraway seeds
salt and freshly ground
black pepper**

Dice potatoes and cook in boiling water for 5 minutes until just tender. Meanwhile, heat the oil in a large frying pan. Add the onion and fry for 5 minutes, stirring occasionally until softened but not browned.

Drain the potatoes and add to the frying pan with the butter, cabbage and cooked meat. Sprinkle the caraway seeds over and season well. Cover and cook for 5 minutes, stirring once or twice until the cabbage has softened.

Remove the lid, increase the heat and cook for 5 minutes more, stirring frequently until browned.

COOK'S NOTE
Diced ready-cooked potatoes can be substituted for the new potatoes if you prefer.

GARLIC GRILLED TOMATOES

Serves 4
40 Calories a portion

**4 tomatoes
1 clove garlic, crushed
salt and coarsely ground
black pepper
1 tbsp olive oil**

Halve the tomatoes and arrange in a shallow ovenproof dish. Sprinkle the garlic and seasoning over and drizzle with oil.

Grill for 5 minutes until hot and lightly browned.

PLUM AND ALMOND CRUMBLE

Serves 4
450 Calories a portion

**550g (1.¼lb) plums, halved
and stoned
100g (4oz) soft light Muscovado
sugar
75g (3oz) plain flour
25g (1oz) rolled oats
50g (2oz) butter, diced
50g (2oz) ground almonds
2 tbsp flaked almonds
TO SERVE:
single cream or ready-made
custard**

Put the plums into the base of a deep 1.1 litre (2 pint) ovenproof dish. Sprinkle with half the sugar.

Put the flour, oats and remaining sugar into a separate bowl or food processor. Add the butter and rub in or process to make fine crumbs. Stir in the ground almonds then spoon over the plums and level the surface.

Sprinkle with the flaked almonds. Cook for 25-30 minutes at 190°C (375°F) gas 5 until golden, covering with foil after 20 minutes if over browning. Serve with cream or custard if liked.

ON YOUR MARKS. . .

● *Preheat the oven to 190°C (375°F) gas 5*

● *Make the crumble, then put in the oven to cook*

● *Blanch the potatoes and prepare the hash browns*

● *Halve and cook the tomatoes*

● *Leave the crumble to finish cooking while you serve the main course*

Hash Browns with Garlic Grilled Tomatoes; Plum and Almond Crumble to follow

SIMPLE FISH SUPPER

The lightest and simplest of lemony fish dishes followed by a refreshing duo of oranges and kiwi fruit in a ginger syrup

Lemon Glazed Haddock with Caper Sauce

New Potatoes, Courgettes and French Beans

Sunshine Salad

TIMEPLAN FOR SERVING SUPPER AT 7.30PM

7.00 Prepare Sunshine Salad.

7.10 Put a pan of water on for the potatoes. Wash potatoes and courgettes. Put potatoes on to cook and steam the courgettes and frozen beans on top.

7.15 Preheat grill. Line grill pan with foil, brush fish with butter, oil and lemon mixture and put under the grill.

7.20 Make caper sauce. Put tomatoes under grill.

7.25 Drain potatoes and put into a serving dish. Toss courgettes and beans in butter and put into a serving dish.

7.30 Garnish haddock with tomato and lemon and serve.

Lemon Glazed Haddock with Caper Sauce, with boiled new potatoes, French beans and courgettes, followed by Sunshine Salad

LEMON GLAZED HADDOCK WITH CAPER SAUCE

The best way to cook fish is often the simplest – and cooking 4 fillets under the grill is easier than managing them in a frying pan.
Serves 4
305 Calories a portion

4 haddock fillets, weighing about 175-250g (6-8oz) each
25g (1oz) butter, melted
1 tbsp oil
½ a lemon, grated rind and
1 tbsp juice
2 firm tomatoes, each cut into
6 wedges
salt and freshly ground
black pepper
lemon slices, to garnish
SAUCE:
4 tbsp plain yogurt
2 tbsp mayonnaise
1 tbsp capers, coarsely chopped

Place the haddock in a grill pan lined with foil. Mix together the butter, oil, lemon rind and juice then use to brush over the fish.

Grill the fish on a high setting for 5-6 minutes. (It does not need turning over.) Put the tomato wedges on the grill pan for the final 2 minutes – just to warm them through.

Meanwhile, mix together the yogurt, mayonnaise and capers and put in a sauce boat.

Season the fish well, then serve immediately, garnished with tomato wedges and slices of lemon.

Serve the sauce separately. Accompany the haddock with small boiled new potatoes, steamed courgettes and French beans tossed in butter.

SUNSHINE SALAD

A very refreshing, fruity, full-of-Vitamin-C dessert, with a subtle hint of ginger.
Serves 4
75 Calories a portion

3 oranges
2 kiwi fruits
1 large piece stem ginger in syrup, finely chopped
2-3 tsp syrup, from stem ginger jar
ginger thins, for serving (optional)

Cut the peel off the oranges and segment them with a sharp knife, catching all the juice from them in a serving bowl. Put the orange segments in the bowl.

Peel and slice the kiwi fruits, or cut them into wedges, and add to the orange segments.

Stir in the ginger and syrup carefully so that the fruit is not broken up. Serve in small glass dishes and accompany with ginger thins, if liked.

WINE CHOICE
The haddock needs an inexpensive rustic white: a vin de pays *with a bit of substance, from Haute Poitou, Charente or the Côtes de Gascogne. For the dessert, choose a sweet, golden wine from California or Australia (look for the grape variety, orange muscat, on the label), which will match the orange flavour and rich spiciness of the fruit.*

SPEEDY FAMILY SUPPER

Ring the changes with this exotic meal that all the family are sure to enjoy

*Pork with Sage
and Mustard*

*Peas with Lettuce and
Spring Onions*

Buttered New Potatoes

Raspberry Ratafia Crush

PORK WITH SAGE AND MUSTARD

Boneless pork chops are now becoming widely available from supermarkets and are much quicker to cook than traditional chops with bones. Combined with sage, mustard and cider, this makes a quick evening meal that's deliciously different from just serving them grilled.
Serves 4
330 Calories a portion

25g (1oz) butter or 1 tbsp oil
4 boneless pork chops
1-2 tbsp fresh chopped sage, or
1 tsp dried
1-2 tbsp wholegrain mustard
300ml (½pint) dry cider
salt and freshly ground
black pepper
fresh sage sprig, to garnish

Heat the butter or oil in a frying pan then fry the chops over a high heat to seal each side. Turn down the heat, add the chopped sage then cook for about 5 minutes more on each side or until tender.

Arrange on a warm serving platter then add the mustard, cider and seasoning to the pan. Boil rapidly until reduced by half then pour over the chops and garnish with the sage. Hand round any remaining sauce separately. Serve with new potatoes, tossed in black pepper and butter, and Peas with Lettuce and Spring Onions.

PEAS WITH LETTUCE AND SPRING ONIONS

Serves 4
50 Calories a portion

Boil frozen petit pois according to the instructions on the packet. Just before the end of cooking time add 1 small chopped round lettuce and 6 chopped spring onions. Drain and serve with a knob of butter.

RASPBERRY RATAFIA CRUSH

This scrumptious dessert is made with raspberries, almond-tasting ratafias and crème fraîche (see Cook's Note). Alternatively, use lightly whipped whipping cream or Greek yogurt.
Serves 4
190 Calories a portion

175g (6oz) raspberries, thawed
if frozen
150ml (5fl oz) crème fraîche
2 tbsp raspberry jam
16 ratafia biscuits, lightly crushed

Reserve 12 of the raspberries then fold the remainder into the crème fraîche with the jam and three quarters of the ratafia biscuits. Spoon into small glasses then pile on remaining raspberries and biscuits.
Serve chilled.

COOK'S NOTE
Crème fraîche is a lightly soured cream from France. It's now more widely available in supermarkets, but if you're unable to buy it you can make something very similar by mixing equal quantities of soured cream and lightly whipped whipping cream.

TIMEPLAN FOR SERVING SUPPER AT 7.30PM

7.00 *Make the Raspberry Ratafia Crush dessert then chill until ready to serve.*
7.10 *Put two pans of salted water on to boil. Meanwhile prepare the potatoes.*
7.15 *Melt the butter then start to cook the chops with the sage.*
7.20 *Put the potatoes and peas on to cook. Then prepare the spring onions and lettuce.*
7.25 *Add the lettuce and onions to the peas, then turn off the heat.*
7.26 *Arrange the chops on a serving platter and garnish with the sage.*
7.27 *Add the cider and mustard to the pork juices in the pan then boil rapidly to reduce.*
7.30 *Spoon the sauce over the meat and serve with the vegetables.*

Pork with Sage and Mustard, Peas with Lettuce and Spring Onions, then Raspberry Ratafia Crush to follow

AN ORIENTAL MEAL

A simple meal with an Oriental flavour

Stir-fried Beef in Black
Bean Sauce

Coconut Rice

Three-fruit Salad with
Ginger

STIR-FRIED BEEF IN BLACK BEAN SAUCE

Serves 4
265 Calories a portion

2 tbsp oil
½ tbsp finely chopped fresh root ginger
225g (8 oz) quick-fry beef, cut into strips
1 red pepper, deseeded and cut into 'matchsticks'
8 spring onions, trimmed and shredded
425g (15oz) can baby sweetcorn, drained, and halved if large
225g (8oz) beansprouts, rinsed
160g (5.½oz) bottle black bean sauce (see Cook's Note)

Heat the oil in a large frying pan or wok. Add the ginger and beef and stir-fry for just a few seconds until the meat is brown. Add the red pepper and spring onions. Stir-fry for about a minute more. Finally add the sweetcorn, beansprouts and black bean sauce.
Not suitable for freezing.

COOK'S NOTE
Stir-fry sauces are a quick way of adding an authentic Oriental flavour. They come in a range of flavours from the familiar sweet and sour to the more unusual black bean – made from small black soya beans fermented with salt and spices. They're available from large supermarkets and Chinese food stores.

ON YOUR MARKS. . .
- Prepare the fruit salad then chill until ready to serve
- Put the rice on to cook with the creamed coconut, cloves, stock and seasoning
- Prepare all the ingredients for the stir-fry
- Heat the oil and start stir-frying the beef. Add the vegetables then coat in the sauce
- Serve the stir-fry immediately. The rice should be ready to serve at the same time

Stir-fried Beef in Black Bean Sauce, Coconut Rice then Three-fruit Salad with Ginger

COCONUT RICE

Serves 4
315 Calories a portion

225g (8oz) white long grain rice
50g (2oz) creamed coconut
2 cloves
575ml (1pint) chicken stock
salt and freshly ground black pepper
flat leaf parsley, to garnish

Put all the ingredients in a large pan, bring to the boil then cover and reduce the heat. Simmer for 15-20 minutes or until the rice is tender and the liquid has been absorbed. Serve immediately, garnished with parsley.
Not suitable for freezing.

THREE-FRUIT SALAD WITH GINGER

Serves 4
130 Calories a portion

425g (15oz) can lychees in syrup
2 kiwi fruit, peeled, halved and sliced
175g (6oz) black grapes, halved and seeded
2 pieces stem ginger (from a jar in syrup), shredded

Pour the lychees with their syrup into a bowl. Add the remaining fruit, then spoon into individual glasses and top with the shredded ginger. Chill until ready to serve.
Not suitable for freezing.

CARIBBEAN SUPPER

Take a trip to the Caribbean for prawns in a lively chilli sauce
followed by a tempting, colourful fruit dessert

PRAWNS IN CREOLE SAUCE

Serves 4
510 Calories a portion

1 tbsp olive oil
1 clove garlic, crushed
1 onion, sliced
1 green pepper, deseeded and
sliced into strips
2 tsp capers
500g (1lb) frozen peeled prawns,
thawed and drained
400g (14oz) can chopped
tomatoes
2 tbsp chilli relish
1 tsp brown sugar
salt and freshly ground
black pepper
¼ tsp Tabasco
8 black olives (optional)
2 tbsp freshly chopped parsley or
chives, to garnish (optional)
RICE:
250-300g (8-10oz) quick-cook
American rice
1 tsp each paprika and
ground coriander

Cook the rice, according to the directions on the packet, for 15 minutes. Heat the olive oil in a large frying pan and sauté the garlic, onion and green pepper for about 3 minutes, stirring gently.

Stir in the capers and prawns and stir-fry for 2-3 minutes. Add the tomatoes, relish, sugar, seasoning and Tabasco. Simmer, uncovered, stirring occasionally, for 10-12 minutes to let the sauce thicken a little. Stir in the olives, if using.

When all the water has been absorbed into the rice, stir in the paprika and coriander, then spoon the cooked rice on to a large warm serving dish. Spoon the prawn mixture onto the warm serving dish alongside the Spicy Rice, garnish with parsley or chives if liked and serve immediately.

TO SERVE: accompany with a simple frisée (curly endive) salad with a lemon and hazelnut dressing. To make the dressing, whisk together 1 tablespoon of hazelnut oil and 2 tablespoons of olive oil with 1 tablespoon of fresh lemon juice and a pinch of salt, pepper and sugar.

FRUIT CREATION

Arranging fruits on a 'puddle' of fruit sauce can look very stylish and artistic but is in fact extremely simple – and most refreshing as well as being low in calories.
Serves 4
120 Calories a portion

425g (15oz) can mangoes in syrup
250g (8oz) small strawberries,
hulled
2 small bananas
a little lemon juice
2 tbsp chopped pecan nuts or
walnuts, toasted

Purée the mangoes with half the syrup in a processor or blender. Add a little extra syrup if it's not smooth enough. Divide the purée carefully between 4 dessert plates, tilting them to let the purée settle in a neat circle on each plate.

Cut the strawberries in half (or slice if large) and the bananas into neat oblique slices. Toss these in a little lemon juice. Arrange the strawberries and bananas on the purée and sprinkle with chopped toasted pecan nuts or walnuts.

Prawns in Creole Sauce

Spicy Rice

Frisée Salad

Fruit Creation

ON YOUR MARKS...

● *Heat grill and toast nuts*

● *Purée mangoes*

● *Prepare fruits for dessert*

● *Put rice on to cook. Follow directions on packet – it should take about 15 minutes*

● *Start cooking Creole sauce*

● *Spoon mango purée on to dessert plates and arrange fruits on top*

● *Wash frisée leaves and shake dry. Place in a salad bowl and sprinkle with lemon juice and hazelnut oil*

● *Stir spices into cooked rice. (All the cooking water should have been absorbed.) Spoon on to a hot serving dish*

● *Add optional black olives to the Creole sauce*

● *Spoon prawn mixture on to serving dish, garnish and serve. Sprinkle toasted, chopped nuts on dessert just before serving*

Prawns in Creole Sauce with spicy rice and frisée salad followed by Fruit Creation

A CHINESE MEAL

Don't sacrifice taste for speed when you need a quick meal.
Try lemony chicken with Chinese noodles, followed by fruit-topped ice-cream

LEMON AND CORIANDER CHICKEN

Serves 4
185 Calories a portion

4 boned chicken breasts, skinned
2 tbsp plain flour
1 tbsp oil
1.½-2 tbsp chopped fresh
coriander
300ml (½pint) chicken stock
2 tbsp lemon juice
salt and freshly ground
black pepper
lemon wedges, sprigs of fresh
coriander, to garnish
(optional)

Coat the chicken breasts in the flour, reserve any remaining for thickening the sauce.

Heat the oil in a large frying pan. Add the chicken and cook on both sides until golden. Blend the coriander and remaining flour into the stock and lemon juice then pour into the pan; cook for 5-10 minutes more until the chicken is tender and the sauce has thickened. Season to taste.

Garnish with lemon wedges and coriander, if liked.

Serve with the Sesame Noodles and an attractive selection of lightly cooked fresh vegetables such as French beans, mangetout and shredded leeks.

SESAME NOODLES

Serves 4
290 Calories a portion

Cook a 300g (10oz) packet of Chinese egg noodles according to the packet instructions.

Meanwhile fry a tablespoon of finely chopped fresh root ginger in a tablespoon of sesame oil with a tablespoon of sesame seeds. Drain the noodles and add to the pan with a tablespoon of soy sauce. Toss together until all the noodles are well coated.

Serve immediately with the Lemon and Coriander Chicken.

VANILLA ICE WITH BLACKBERRY AND PASSION FRUIT SAUCE

Serves 4
225 Calories a portion

213g (7.½oz) can unsweetened
blackberries in fruit juice
2 tsp cornflour
1 passion fruit
1 tbsp sugar
8 scoops vanilla ice cream
crisp biscuits, to serve (optional)

Drain blackberry juice into a pan then blend in cornflour. Heat gently, stirring until thickened. Remove from heat and pour into a serving bowl.
Stir in the blackberries and the pulp and seeds from the passion fruit. Sweeten with the sugar.

Just before serving, pile scoops of the ice cream into serving glasses and spoon over the sauce. Accompany with the biscuits, if liked.

Lemon and Coriander Chicken

Sesame Noodles

Vanilla Ice with Blackberry and Passion Fruit Sauce

ON YOUR MARKS. . .

- *Make the blackberry and passion fruit sauce. Cover with clear film to prevent a skin forming, then set aside*

- *Coat the chicken breasts with flour. Heat the oil then fry the chicken until golden*

- *Put the noodles on to cook. Meanwhile chop the ginger and prepare the vegetables*

- *Add the remaining ingredients to the chicken and leave to complete the cooking time*

- *Put the vegetables on to boil in lightly salted water*

- *Fry the sesame seeds and ginger, drain the noodles, add to the pan and toss well with the soy sauce*

- *Serve the chicken with the noodles and vegetables*

- *Scoop the ice cream into bowls and pour over the blackberry and passion fruit sauce just before serving*

Lemon and Coriander Chicken, Sesame Noodles and Vanilla Ice with Blackberry and Passion Fruit Sauce

SIMPLE ITALIAN-STYLE SUPPER

Fish baked in the oven with cheese and ham, served with warm crusty bread
and a refreshing salad...to follow, a delicious pineapple dessert –
and who would believe it only took minutes?

Pizza Topped Cod

Salad Italian Style

Pineapple Almondine

PIZZA TOPPED COD

Serves 4
175 Calories a portion

6 tomatoes, sliced
4 cod steaks or cutlets
125g (4oz) mature Cheddar cheese, grated
2 slices ham, cut into strips
3 or 4 black olives (optional)
freshly ground black pepper

Arrange the tomatoes in a shallow baking dish. Place the cod on top then scatter with the cheese. Criss-cross the ham to make a lattice over the cheese. Dot with olives if using, then grind over some black pepper. Bake at 200°C (400°F) gas 6 for 20 minutes until the cheese melts.

SALAD ITALIAN STYLE

Serves 4
40 Calories a portion

Shred half each of an iceberg lettuce and frisée (curly endive) and place in a salad bowl with sliced cucumber, onion and a green pepper. Just before serving toss in a few table-spoons of Italian dressing and season with salt and freshly ground black pepper to taste.

PINEAPPLE ALMONDINE

Serves 4
165 Calories a portion

1 small fresh pineapple
2 tbsp Amaretto di Saronno (almond liqueur), (optional)
2 tbsp soft brown sugar
2 tbsp flaked almonds

Cut the pineapple into quarters lengthwise and cut away the core. Loosen the pineapple flesh from the skin with a sharp knife and cut into bite-sized pieces, still keeping the quarters whole.

Spoon over the Amaretto, if using, then sprinkle with the sugar and flaked almonds. Bake in the oven at 200°C (400°F) gas 6 for 15 minutes until the nuts brown and the sugar begins to caramelise. Arrange the pineapple shells on individual plates. Serve immediately.

ON YOUR MARKS. . .

- Set the oven to 200°C (400°F) gas 6

- Make the Pizza Topped Cod then put in the oven to cook

- Slice the ingredients for the salad, but don't add the dressing. Chill until ready to serve

- Wrap some crusty bread in foil and put in the oven to warm with the dinner plates

- Prepare the pineapple and put to one side

- Add the dressing to the salad, toss well then serve with the fish and warmed bread

- Put the pineapple in the oven. It will cook while you're eating the main course

A really imaginative meal, with not a moment wasted: Pizza Topped Cod with Salad Italian Style, then baked pineapple

STUNNING STIR-FRY

A colourful stir-fry dish makes a tempting main course, accompanied with potatoes cooked in an interesting way. To follow, pears poached in cider and spice with a delicious ginger sauce

Lamb and Leek Stir-fry

Spicy Seeded Potatoes

Pears with Hot Ginger Sauce

LAMB AND LEEK STIR-FRY

Trimmed neck fillet of lamb is now generally available in supermarkets and butchers. It's quick to cook and economical. Boneless lamb leg steaks are a little more expensive.
Serves 4
250 Calories a portion

350g (12oz) lamb neck fillet or boneless leg steaks
2.5cm (1in) piece fresh root ginger, peeled
1 clove garlic, crushed
1 tbsp dry sherry
1 tsp cornflour
freshly ground black pepper
2 leeks, trimmed and washed
1 large spear broccoli, or ½ small cauliflower
1 carrot, peeled
2 tbsp oil

Cut the lamb into very thin slices and place in a bowl. Shred the ginger and add to the lamb with the garlic, sherry and cornflour. Season well with freshly ground black pepper. Mix well and leave to stand while preparing the vegetables.

Slice the leeks thinly. Cut the broccoli or cauliflower into small florets. Cut the carrot into matchsticks. Heat the oil in a wok or large pan. Add the lamb and marinade ingredients and stir-fry for 2 minutes.

Add the prepared vegetables and cook for 2-3 minutes until tender but still crisp. Serve immediately.

SPICY SEEDED POTATOES

With very little extra preparation than for boiling potatoes, this ready-from-the-pan dish makes an interesting and unusual variation for a popular vegetable.
Serves 4
180 Calories a portion

1 tbsp oil
1 tbsp sesame seeds
1 tsp fenugreek seeds
1 tbsp coriander seeds, roughly crushed
675g (1.½lb) potatoes, scrubbed
300ml (½pint) chicken stock
freshly ground black pepper

Heat the oil in a large pan. Fry all the seeds for 1 minute to draw out the flavours.

Cut the potatoes into 2.5cm (1in) cubes. Add to the pan with the stock and plenty of freshly ground pepper. Stir well to mix then cover and simmer gently for 10-15 minutes, by which time all the stock will have evaporated and the potatoes will be tender. Serve immediately.

PEARS WITH HOT GINGER SAUCE

The cooking time for the pears will vary – if soft, 5-10 minutes will be ample.
Serves 4
180 Calories a portion

4 pears
450ml (¾pint) cider
1 cinnamon stick
25g (1oz) butter
2 tbsp light soft brown sugar
2 tbsp syrup from stem ginger jar
1 tbsp lemon juice
2 pieces stem ginger, chopped
pear leaves, to decorate (optional)

Peel the pears. Place in a shallow pan and add the cider and cinnamon stick. Cover the pan and simmer for 15-20 minutes.

For the ginger sauce, place the remaining ingredients in a small saucepan and bring to the boil, stirring occasionally. Boil for 2-3 minutes. Remove from the heat and cool slightly.

Drain the cooked pears and add some of the juice to the sauce. Serve with the sauce poured over pears. Decorate with pear leaves, if using.

ON YOUR MARKS. . .

- *Slice the lamb and leave to stand in the marinade*

- *Prepare the pears and put on to cook*

- *Prepare, then start to cook the potato dish*

- *Prepare all the vegetables for the stir-fry*

- *Start the ginger sauce. Remove the pears from the heat, drain off juice and add to the sauce*

- *Cook the stir-fry. Stir the ginger sauce occasionally*

- *Serve the main course. Keep the ginger sauce warm*

Lamb and Leek Stir-fry, Spicy Seeded Potatoes, followed by Pears with Hot Ginger Sauce

FRENCH-STYLE DINNER FOR FOUR

A French-style chicken dish with cream, apples and brandy, and a fruity dessert

Normandy Chicken

Julienne of Potatoes, Carrots and Beans

Gooseberry Bramble with Sorbet

Normandy Chicken with Julienne of Potatoes, Carrots and Beans

DRINKS CHOICE
Cider is the natural accompaniment but shouldn't be too sweet. Try following the chicken with a trou Normand – a glass of Calvados – to clean the palate. The puckering effect of gooseberry and the powerful flavour of passion fruit need the weight of either a Sauternes or Barsac; or try a sweet Muscat – Frontignan makes a change from Beaumes de Venise (both French).

COOK'S NOTE
Passion fruit sorbet is readlily available in supermarkets and frozen food centres. If however you fancy a change, substitute another complementary flavour.

TIMEPLAN FOR SERVING
DINNER AT 7.30PM

7.00 *Prepare and cook apples in a large frying pan. Then put the apples in a dish in a warm oven. Add the chicken to the pan.*
7.05 *Put gooseberries on to cook. Turn chicken. Prepare potatoes and carrots.*
7.10 *Put a kettle of water on to boil for the vegetables. Add brandy to the frying pan. Cover and simmer for 15 minutes. Drain gooseberries and add bramble or redcurrant jelly to the pan and heat gently. Sweeten if necessary.*
7.15 *Put potatoes and carrots on to cook in a pan of salted water. Pre-heat grill to toast almonds. Spoon the cooked gooseberries into a serving dish.*
7.20 *Add the French beans to the other vegetables, and continue cooking. Toast almonds. Set aside. Take sorbet out of the freezer, put in fridge.*
7.25 *Place chicken pieces on a warm serving plate. Add remaining brandy and cream to the frying pan. Drain vegetables, and place in a serving dish. Pour cream sauce over chicken.*
7.30 *Garnish chicken with the apples and toasted flaked almonds and serve.*

NORMANDY CHICKEN

Chicken thighs can be bought in packs of 8 from major supermarkets and are meaty and economical – so keep some in the freezer!
Serves 4
485 Calories a portion

2 colourful, firm eating apples
40g (1.½oz) butter
1 tsp lemon juice
8 small chicken thighs, skinned
3 tbsp brandy
150ml (¼pint) double cream
salt and freshly ground
black pepper
3 tbsp flaked almonds, toasted

Quarter, core and thinly slice the apples. Melt the butter in a large frying pan, add the lemon juice and stir-fry the apple pieces over a moderate heat for 2 minutes. Remove with a draining spoon and put in a warm oven.

Add the chicken thighs to the pan and cook for 2.½ minutes each side to brown them. Add 2 tablespoons of the brandy. Cover the pan and simmer for 15 minutes.

Remove the chicken and arrange on a warm serving plate. Add the remaining brandy and cream to the pan. Stir well and heat through. Season and spoon over the chicken. Garnish with apples and toasted flaked almonds.

JULIENNE OF POTATOES, CARROTS AND BEANS

A colourful mixed vegetable accompaniment and an unusual way to serve potatoes, cutting them into sticks to match crisp beans and carrots in shape.
Serves 4
130 Calories a portion

500g (1lb) potatoes, unpeeled and cut into 5mm (¼in) thick sticks
250g (8oz) carrots, cut into sticks as above
250g (8oz) frozen French beans (haricots verts)

Cook the potato and carrot sticks for 5 minutes in a pan of simmering salted water. Add the beans, return to the boil and cook for a further 2 minutes until the vegetables are just tender.

Drain the vegetables and serve immediately with the Normandy Chicken.

GOOSEBERRY BRAMBLE WITH SORBET

If using fresh gooseberries, choose small fruit with a pink blush for this dessert. Passion fruit sorbet is a perfect foil for the gooseberries.
Serves 4
125 Calories a portion

250g (8oz) fresh gooseberries, topped and tailed (or frozen or bottled gooseberries)
150ml (¼pint) water
3 tbsp bramble or redcurrant jelly
a little sugar for sweetening
8 scoops or slices of passion fruit sorbet (See Cook's Note)
shortbread biscuits (petticoat tails), for serving

Put the fresh gooseberries and water in a pan, bring to the boil and simmer for about 5 minutes. Drain off the water. For frozen fruit, just heat through to thaw, then drain. For bottled fruit, drain off the syrup and do not pre-cook.

Add the jelly to the pan and heat gently, shaking the pan to dissolve the jelly and not break up the fruit. Sweeten if necessary.

Allow the Gooseberry Bramble to cool a little then serve spooned over the scoops of passion fruit sorbet. Accompany with shortbread petticoat tail biscuits.

Refreshing Gooseberry Bramble with Sorbet

AN ITALIAN MEAL FOR FOUR

Treat family or friends to a taste of Italy with this delicious meal

Parma Ham with Melon
(Prosciutto con Melone)

**Pasta with
Tuna and Mushrooms**
(Farfalle con Tonno e Funghi)

Tomato Salad
(Insalata di Pomodori)

Almond Stuffed Peaches
(Pesche alla Piemontese)

PARMA HAM
WITH MELON

*A refreshing starter using
prosciutto, a thinly sliced Italian
ham with a delicate slightly sweet
flavour. As an alternative serve the
melon in wedges with the ham
wrapped round.*
Serves 4
65 Calories a portion

4 slices prosciutto cured ham
1 small honeydew or ogen melon
freshly ground black pepper

Place slices of ham in the centre of
4 individual plates.

Cut the melon into quarters,
remove the seeds then cut off the
rind as evenly as you can. Cut each
quarter diagonally into thin slices.

Arrange melon slices on either
side of the ham on the plate.
Sprinkle with pepper.

Parma Ham with Melon and
Pasta with Tuna and Mushrooms

PASTA WITH TUNA AND MUSHROOMS

Use mature Cheddar cheese if you don't have Parmesan.
Serves 4
595 Calories a portion

375g (12oz) pasta bows (farfalle)
salt and freshly ground
black pepper
1 tsp oil
25g (1oz) butter
6 spring onions, trimmed
and chopped
2 large courgettes, sliced
175g (6oz) button mushrooms,
halved
175ml (6fl oz) milk
1 tbsp flour
198g (7oz) can tuna chunks in
brine, drained
50g (2oz) Parmesan cheese,
grated
142ml (5fl oz) carton single cream

Add the pasta to a large pan of boiling salted water, with a little oil added. Simmer, covered, for about 12 minutes until it is *al dente* (still has a little 'bite').

Meanwhile, melt the butter in a large pan, add the spring onions, courgettes and mushrooms and sauté for 3-4 minutes, stirring occasionally. Remove the vegetables with a draining spoon to a plate.

Whisk the milk with the flour, pour into the pan and bring to the boil, stirring, to make a smooth sauce. Add the tuna and cheese. Stir in the cooked vegetables and cream just before serving. Taste and season well. Drain the pasta and stir carefully into the tuna and cheese sauce until it is just coated.

Spoon on to a warmed serving dish and sprinkle with black pepper.
TO SERVE: accompany with a tomato salad Cut 4 tomatoes in wedges or slices and put into a shallow bowl. Sprinkle with 1 tbsp olive or walnut oil and 1-2 tsp freshly chopped basil, oregano, parsley or chives or spring onion tops. Season to taste.

ALMOND STUFFED PEACHES

Italians aren't great ones for desserts, however this simple recipe is quite heavenly.
Serves 4
270 Calories a portion (without ice cream)

411g (14½oz) can peach halves in
syrup, drained, reserving syrup
75g (3oz) pack ratafias or
macaroons, lightly crushed
50g (2oz) plain chocolate
polka dots
25g (1oz) flaked almonds
15g (½oz) butter
vanilla Italian ice cream, to serve
(optional)

Arrange the peach halves, cut side up, in a shallow ovenproof dish.

Mix the ratafias or macaroons with the chocolate, 3 tablespoons peach syrup and the almonds.

Spoon the mixture over the peaches and dot with the butter.

Sprinkle with 3 tablespoons peach syrup. Bake at 180°C (350°F) gas 4 for 20-30 minutes until the top is browned and the chocolate is almost melted. Serve warm with scoops of ice cream.

WINE CHOICE
White wine will suit the whole meal perfectly, and none better than a delicate Südtirol (or South Tyrol) Chardonnay to start with. Something a little fuller would stand up better with the pasta: dry Orvieto, or Vernaccia di San Gimignano from central Italy. If you prefer red, make it a lightweight one such as Bardolino or Valpolicella. Finish in the only way possible, with an Asti or Moscato Spumante, which is light in alcohol, sweetly grapy, but refreshing too.

TIMEPLAN FOR SERVING THE MEAL AT 8.00PM

7.30 Set oven temperature at 180°C (350°F) gas 4. Prepare the peach dessert.
7.40 Put a large pan of salted water on to boil for the pasta. Prepare the starter and place ready on the table.
7.45 Make the tomato salad. Prepare the vegetables for the pasta sauce and start to sauté. Grate cheese.
7.55 Put pasta on to boil. Make the sauce, adding just the tuna and cheese.
8.00 Put the peaches in the oven and set the timer for 20 minutes. Start the meal.
When ready to serve the main course, drain pasta and add to the sauce with the vegetables and cream. Heat through. Serve on a warm platter. Remove peaches from the oven. Serve warm.

Almond Stuffed Peaches - a classic Italian dessert

EXOTIC FAMILY MEAL

Here's an exotic meal that all the family are sure to love

Chicken with Almonds and Raisins

Lemony Rice

Tomato and Cucumber Vinaigrette

Banana Coffee Creams

CHICKEN WITH ALMONDS AND RAISINS

Chicken is a popular choise for mid-week meals so here's a recipe that transforms it into somthing a little different. Boneless portions are coated in flour and spices then cooked with crunchy almonds, raisins and lemon. Don't waste the lemon rind - stir it into the boiled rice accompaniment for a really refreshing flavour.
Serves 4
325 Calories per portion

2 tbsp plain flour
1 tsp ground turmeric
2 tsp ground coriander
salt and freshly ground
black pepper
4 small boneless chicken breasts
(suprêmes)
25g (1oz) butter or 1 tbsp oil
40g (1½ oz) whole blanched
almonds
40g (1½oz) raisins
1 lemon, grated rind and juice

Mix together the flour, spices and seasoning then use to coat the chicken breasts.

Heat the butter or oil in a large frying pan then cook the almonds until golden. Lift out the almonds then cook the chicken, covered on each side for 5 - 8 minutes.

Add the raisins and lemon juice then cook for 5 minutes more or until the chicken is cooked through.

Arrange on a bed of the Lemony Rice and scatter over the almonds.

LEMONY RICE

Serves 4
225 Calories a portion

Boil 300g (10oz) Basmati or ordinary long-grain rice for 10-15 minutes or until tender.

Drain then add the grated rind of a lemon and plenty of seasoning.

TOMATO AND CUCUMBER VINAIGRETTE

Serves 4
75 Calories a portion

Slice 500g (1lb) ripe tomatoes. Peel and dice half a cucumber then toss both vegetables in three tablespoons of French dressing.

Season with salt and plenty of freshly ground black pepper.

BANANA COFFEE CREAMS

Creamy Greek yogurt, banana and coffee makes this quick to put together dessert.

Serves 4
230 Calories a portion

3 ripe bananas
1tbsp instant coffee powder
1 tbsp soft brown sugar
450g (1lb) tub Greek yogurt
extra coffee powder for sprinkling

Slice two of the bananas - reserve eight slices for decoration then place the remainder into the base of four glasses.

Mash the third banana then mix with the coffee powder, sugar and all but eight teaspoonfuls of the yogurt.

Spoon into glasses then top with the reserved yogurt and sliced banana. Sprinkle with coffee then chill before serving.

Chicken with Almonds and Raisins with Lemony Rice and Tomato and Cucumber Vinaigrette followed by Banana Coffee Creams

AN IMPRESSIVE QUICK MEAL

Here's an ingenious main meal that makes the most
of popular lamb steaks and seasonal vegetables

**Lamb with Mint and
Cranberry Glaze**

**Potato and Sprout Purée
with Cheese and Nutmeg**

**Shredded Leeks with
Poppy Seeds**

Buttered Carrots

LAMB WITH MINT AND CRANBERRY GLAZE

Serves 4
425 Calories a portion

**½ tbsp oil
4 medium or 8 small prime
chump lamb steaks, trimmed
of fat
3 tbsp cranberry sauce
1 tbsp cornflour
1 tbsp fresh chopped mint or
½ tsp dried
300ml (½ pint) lamb or
chicken stock
salt and freshly ground
black pepper
sprigs of fresh mint, to garnish**

Heat the oil, add the lamb steaks
then cook for a few minutes until
browned on both sides.

Blend the cranberry sauce, cornflour and mint into the stock, season,
then pour into the pan. Allow to bubble then turn down the heat and
cook gently for about 10 minutes.
Garnish with sprigs of fresh mint just
before serving.

POTATO AND SPROUT PURÉE WITH CHEESE AND NUTMEG

Serves 4
175 Calories a portion

**450g (1lb) potatoes, peeled and diced
250g (9oz) Brussels sprouts,
fresh and trimmed or frozen
salt and freshly ground
black pepper
large knob of butter
good pinch freshly grated nutmeg
50g (2oz) Cheddar cheese, grated**

Cook the potatoes and sprouts in
boiling salted water for about 15 minutes until tender. Drain then mash
with the seasoning, butter and nutmeg to taste.

Spoon into a heatproof dish, sprinkle with cheese and grill.

SHREDDED LEEKS WITH POPPY SEEDS

Serves 4
35 Calories a portion

**2 leeks
1 tbsp olive oil
1 tbsp poppy seeds
salt and freshly ground
black pepper**

Halve the leeks lengthways then
wash under cold running water to
remove any grit. Drain then slice the
leeks into long thin strips.

Heat the oil in a large frying pan,
add the poppy seeds and fry for
about 30 seconds. Add the leeks,
season to taste then stir fry for about
5 minutes until the leeks are tender

BUTTERED CARROTS

Scrape or peel 350g (12oz) carrots
and cut into fingers. Steam for about
10-15 minutes until they are just tender. Then add seasoning and butter
to taste.

**Tasty lamb steaks and spiced
vegetables followed by fresh
fruit, cheese and biscuits**

ON YOUR MARKS. . .

- Put a pan of salted water on to boil for the potatoes and sprouts, prepare the vegetables and put them on to cook

- Wash and shred the leeks. Peel and cut the carrots into fingers

- Put the lamb on to cook and blend the sauce

- Put a pan of water on to boil for the carrots

- Drain and mash the potatoes and sprouts. Complete the dish and grill

- Add the sauce to the lamb and leave to cook

- Put the carrots on to steam

- Stir fry the shredded leeks with the poppy seeds

- Serve. Complete the meal with fresh fruit, cheese and biscuits or yogurt

SPECIAL TURKEY MEAL

For a special supper or lunch this turkey meal will go down a real treat

Turkey with Tarragon Sauce

Sesame Potatoes

French-style Peas

Nectarine Cointreau Surprise

TURKEY WITH TARRAGON SAUCE

Serves 4
210 Calories a portion

25g (1oz) butter
1 tbsp sunflower oil
4 turkey breast escalopes
1 bunch spring onions, sliced
150g (5oz) button mushrooms, wiped and sliced
4 tbsp dry vermouth
1 tbsp freshly chopped tarragon
salt and freshly ground black pepper
1 tsp cornflour
175g (6oz) natural yogurt
fresh tarragon, to garnish (optional)

Heat the butter and oil together in a large frying pan. Add the turkey escalopes and cook for 3-4 minutes each side, depending on their thickness, until browned.

Add the onions and mushrooms to pan and cook for a further 3 minutes. Remove the escalopes from the pan and place on a warmed platter.

Add the vermouth, chopped tarragon and seasoning to the mushroom mixture and cook for 2 minutes until the vermouth has reduced a little.

Mix the cornflour and yogurt together. Take the pan off the heat and stir in the yogurt mix. Return to the heat and bring the sauce just to the boil, stirring. Spoon over the escalopes and garnish with the extra tarragon if liked.

SESAME POTATOES

Serves 4
110 Calories a portion

575g (1.¼lb) ready-scrubbed baby new potatoes
salt
25g (1oz) butter
1 tbsp sesame seeds

Cook the potatoes in boiling, salted water for 15 minutes.

Drain. Heat the butter in the drained pan. Add the sesame seeds and fry for about 1 minute until beginning to colour. Add the potatoes and toss together.

FRENCH-STYLE PEAS

Serves 4
70 Calories a portion

275g (10oz) frozen petits pois
2 tomatoes
15g (½oz) butter
½ iceberg lettuce, leaves separated and washed
pinch of sugar
salt and freshly ground black pepper

Cook petits pois in boiling water for 2 minutes. Drain and set aside.

Cut the tomatoes into thin wedges. Heat the butter in the drained pan and fry the tomatoes for 2 minutes until just softened.

Shred the lettuce and add to the pan with the peas, sugar and seasoning. Cook for 1 minute.
Serve immediately

NECTARINE COINTREAU SURPRISE

Serves 4
170 Calories a portion

25g (1oz) butter
6 nectarines, stoned and sliced
2 tbsp demerara sugar
2 tbsp Cointreau
cream or fromage frais, to serve (optional)

Heat the butter in a frying pan, add the nectarines and sugar and cook for 2 minutes, stirring occasionally.

Add the Cointreau and cook for 1 minute. Spoon into serving dishes. Top with cream or fromage frais.

ON YOUR MARKS. . .

● *Put a saucepan of water on to boil, ready to cook the potatoes*

● *Prepare the nectarines for the dessert, but don't cook them*

● *Fry the turkey escalopes then set aside while finishing the tarragon sauce*

● *Cook the peas and add the lettuce just before serving*

● *Drain the potatoes and sprinkle with sesame seeds*

● *Serve the main course*

● *The dessert can be quickly sautéed just before serving*

Turkey with Tarragon Sauce and tasty vegetables; Nectarine Cointreau Surprise to finish

A SPECIAL OCCASION BRUNCH

A brunch menu with a choice to start. Make up quantities to suit the number, ages and preferences of your party

ON YOUR MARKS...

- *Preheat oven to 200°C (400°F) gas 6*

- *Prepare number of grapefruit required and put in fridge to chill*

- *Prepare quantity of milkshake required, cover and chill*

- *Prepare bread for toasted cups then put in oven to bake*

- *Make up lemon and cranberry spreads and place in serving dishes*

- *Put milk (and water) and drinking chocolate into a pan*

- *Make Cheese and Apple Scramble. Remove pan from heat and cover to keep warm*

- *Serve grapefruit and milkshakes*

- *Serve cheese and apple scramble in toasted cups. Turn down oven and put bakery selection in to warm*

- *Heat chocolate, boil briefly and serve with bakeries and spreads*

A really delicious brunch for a special occasion

Strawberry and Passion Fruit Milkshake

Grapefruit Miller Howe

Cheese and Apple Scramble in Toasted Cups

Bakery Selection with Lemony and Cranberry Toppings

Hot Chocolate

using a serrated grapefruit knife, cut round the inside edge and divide up into sections. Pour 1 teaspoon crème de menthe over each and toss sections around, piling the fruit up towards the centre.

Serve chilled, garnished with sprigs of mint and sitting on fern leaves for a professional look.

COOK'S NOTE
Look out for pink grapefruit — they're sweeter tasting than the yellow ones and don't need sugar.

BAKERY SELECTION WITH LEMONY AND CRANBERRY TOPPINGS

By way of a change from the usual preserves, make up this quick lemon cheese and chunky cranberry and orange relish for spreading on your choice of 'breads'.
Serves 4-6
Variable calories (croissants are highest in calories)

selection of crumpets, croissants, scotch pancakes and/or waffles
200g (7oz) soft cheese
2 tbsp lemon curd
1 seedless orange
½-¾small jar cranberry sauce

Put bakery selection in the oven to warm for 10-15 minutes at 140°C (275°F) gas 1. Blend soft cheese with lemon curd and put in a serving dish. Cut peel and pith away from orange, chop flesh then stir into cranberry sauce and put in another dish. Serve both, for spreading together on chosen bakeries.

STRAWBERRY AND PASSION FRUIT MILKSHAKE

A fruit yogurt adds a contrasting flavour to jam and gives a creamy smooth consistency. Any flavour yogurt and jam can be used.
Serves 2
205 Calories a glass

300ml (½pint) milk
150g (5oz) carton passion fruit yogurt
2 tbsp strawberry jam

Thoroughly blend together milk, yogurt and jam in a jug. Serve chilled with straws.

GRAPEFRUIT MILLER HOWE

This is how chef John Tovey, of the Miller Howe Hotel on Lake Windermere, likes to serve grapefruit – sprinkled with crème de menthe. Strictly one for adults.
Serves 2
30 Calories a portion

1 grapefruit (see Cook's Note)
2 tsp crème de menthe
sprigs of fresh mint, to garnish

Cut grapefruit in half, making 'V' shaped cuts around the skin. Then

CHEESE AND APPLE SCRAMBLE

Scrambled eggs are popular with all ages but as this is a 'brunch' make them more substantial with tasty cheese and crisp apples.
Serves 4-6
520-410 Calories a portion

8-12 slices wholemeal bread
butter paper, for greasing
large knob of butter
9 eggs
4 tbsp milk
salt and ground black pepper
1.½ tsp wholegrain mustard
75g (3oz) mature Cheddar cheese
2 crisp eating apples
watercress or dill, to garnish

Remove crusts from bread and flatten slices slightly with a rolling pin. Grease 8-12 patty tins with butter paper then press a slice of bread firmly into each to form 'cups'. Bake at 200°C (400°F) gas 6 for about 10 minutes until crisp and golden.

Melt butter in a non-stick saucepan. Beat eggs with milk, salt and pepper to taste, and mustard. Tip into pan and cook over a moderate heat. In between stirs, grate cheese, core and dice apples – do not peel. When the eggs are just scrambled, remove pan from heat. Stir in cheese and apples. The mixture should be just set. Serve in toasted 'cups'. Garnish.

HOT CHOCOLATE

Boil milk (or half milk and water) in a saucepan and add drinking chocolate to taste. Allow 200ml (⅓ pint) liquid and 2-3 tsp chocolate per person. Boil briefly, whisking to make frothy, then pour into large breakfast cups and sprinkle with a little powdered drinking chocolate.

A DELICIOUS QUICK MEAL

You don't have to sacrifice taste for speed with this delicious menu. There's succulent pork escalopes in a creamy mushroom sauce, served with pasta and French-style peas, followed by tempting hot rum and raisin bananas

Escalopes with Creamy
Mushroom Sauce

Petits Pois à la Française

Pasta Paprika

Bananas Barbados

Escalopes with Creamy Mushroom Sauce and Pasta Paprika, Petits Pois à la Française; and Bananas Barbados

ESCALOPES WITH CREAMY MUSHROOM SAUCE

Serves 4
345 Calories a portion

2 tbsp plain flour
1 tsp ground paprika
salt and freshly ground
black pepper
4 pork escalopes
25g (1oz) butter
1 tbsp oil
125g (4oz) small mushrooms
150ml (¼pint) double cream or
soured cream
2 tbsp finely chopped chives and
whole chives or spring
onion tops to garnish

Mix the flour, paprika and seasonings then use this mixture to coat the escalopes. Heat the butter and oil in a frying pan and when foaming add the meat. Cook for 3 minutes each side then take out of the pan, arrange on a warm serving plate and keep warm in the oven.

Slice the mushrooms, add to the pan and stir-fry for 2-3 minutes until just turning golden. Pour in the cream stirring continuously until the sauce bubbles and starts to thicken. Add the chopped chives, check for seasoning, then spoon the sauce over the pork escalopes. Finally garnish with whole chives.

PETITS POIS À LA FRANÇAISE

Serves 4
90 Calories a portion

Put 225g (8oz) of frozen petits pois and 4 spring onions, trimmed and finely sliced, into a pan with 2 tablespoons boiling water, about 25g (1oz) butter and a tablespoon of sugar. Cook, covered, for about 5 minutes, then add 125g (4oz) of shredded iceberg lettuce and cook for another minute until slightly softened. Drain well, spoon into a warm serving dish, season well with salt and freshly ground black pepper. Dot with a little more butter and garnish with fresh mint sprigs, if liked.

PASTA PAPRIKA

Serves 4
240 Calories a portion

Heat up a pan of salted water and cook 225g (8oz) pasta penne, for example, according to the instructions on the packet.

Drain well and toss in a little olive oil, seasoning and a teaspoon of ground paprika.

The pasta should be served immediately in a warm serving dish.

BANANAS BARBADOS

Serves 4
185 Calories a portion

40g (1.½oz) butter
4 bananas peeled and cut into
chunks
1-2 tbsp Muscovado or Barbados
sugar
fresh lemon or lime juice, for
sprinkling
2 tbsp rum
a handful of raisins

Melt the butter in a non-stick frying pan until it starts to foam. Add the bananas and cook over a moderate heat, stirring occasionally for about 2-3 minutes.

Add the remaining ingredients and simmer for 1-2 minutes until syrupy but the bananas still hold their shape. Serve in a warm dish.

AN INFORMAL MEAL WITH FRIENDS

Perfect for family or friends – these deliciously tender lamb cutlets are served with steamed fresh vegetables on a bed of aromatic pilaf rice, and followed with a tempting creamy white chocolate and hazelnut dessert

Lamb Cutlets with Sultana and Ginger Pilaf

Steamed Vegetable Medley

White Chocolate and Hazelnut Creams

ON YOUR MARKS...

- *Make the Chocolate and Hazelnut Creams, then put in the fridge to set*

- *Start the pilaf. While the onions, ginger and garlic are cooking, prepare the vegetables for the accompaniment*

- *Add the rice to the ginger mixture. Stir, add the remaining ingredients, then cover and leave to cook*

- *Put a pan of water on to boil for the vegetables. Place the cutlets under the grill*

- *Cook the vegetables in a steamer over the water (or put in the water and lightly boil)*

- *Serve the main course. Leave the dessert in the fridge until ready to serve*

LAMB CUTLETS WITH SULTANA AND GINGER PILAF

Serves 4
475 Calories a portion

2 tbsp sunflower oil
1 tbsp finely chopped fresh root ginger
1 clove garlic, crushed
1 large onion, chopped
225g (8oz) basmati rice
850ml (1.½pints) vegetable stock
4-5 tbsp sultanas
salt and freshly ground black pepper
8 extra-trimmed lamb cutlets
flat-leaf parsley, to garnish

Heat the oil in a large frying pan, then fry the ginger, garlic and onion until golden. Stir in the rice and toss round the pan for about a minute to coat the grains evenly in oil.

Add the stock, sultanas and seasoning, cover and simmer gently for 15-20 minutes until the stock has been absorbed into the rice and the grains are tender and separate.

Meanwhile grill the cutlets for 8-10 minutes, turning at least once.

Serve the rice on a warmed platter and arrange the chops on top. Garnish with flat-leaf parsley.

STEAMED VEGETABLE MEDLEY

Steam or lightly boil for about 8 minutes a colourful selection of mixed vegetables, such as sliced celery, some fresh baby sweetcorn and halved French beans.

WHITE CHOCOLATE AND HAZELNUT CREAMS

Makes 4
285 Calories each

2 tbsp hazelnuts, chopped
175g (6oz) white chocolate, broken
two 150g (5fl oz) cartons low-fat hazelnut yogurt
1 tbsp Southern Comfort or dark rum (optional)

Place the hazelnuts under the grill for 30 seconds or until golden. Set aside. Put the chocolate in a heatproof bowl, place over a pan of just boiled water, then leave until melted.

Blend in the yogurt until smooth, add the Southern Comfort, or rum, if using. Spoon into small glasses, scatter with the nuts and chill.

Lamb Cutlets with Sultana and Ginger Pilaf, Steamed Vegetable Medley, White Chocolate and Hazelnut Creams

A CELEBRATION DINNER FOR TWO

So often menus are designed for four people. Here's one just for two, although it can be doubled or trebled up and still cooked very quickly

Duck Breasts with Kumquats

Long Grain and Wild Rice

Chicory and Watercress Salad

Chocolate and Chestnut Whip

Duck Breasts with Kumquats with Long Grain and Wild Rice and a Chicory and Watercress Salad followed by Chocolate and Chestnut Whip

ON YOUR MARKS...

- Put water on for the rice
- Melt chocolate for the dessert
- Prepare salad
- Put rice on to cook
- Start cooking the duck dish
- Complete dessert
- Dress salad
- Drain rice, add nuts and put in a covered dish tokeep warm
- Place duck on serving dish and complete sauce
- Pour sauce over duck and serve

DUCK BREASTS WITH KUMQUATS

Duck goes well with fruit flavours and little oval kumquats make an ideal partner. They have a kind of bitter orange taste and because you eat the whole fruit, require no preparation other than slicing.
Serves 2
285 Calories a portion
(without rice)

1 tbsp oil
2 duck breasts (weighing about 175g, 6oz each), skinned
1 clove garlic, crushed
60ml (2fl oz) red wine
25g (1oz) kumquats, sliced
salt and freshly ground black pepper
½ tsp cornflour
1 tbsp orange juice
2 spring onions, sliced diagonally
1 tsp soy sauce
1 tsp clear honey

Heat the oil in a heavy-based pan and fry the duck until sealed. Add the garlic and fry for 1 minute, then add the wine and kumquats with seasoning to taste. Cover and cook for 15 minutes until the duck is tender.

Transfer the duck to a warmed serving dish and keep warm. Blend the cornflour with the orange juice and add to the pan with the spring onions, soy sauce and honey. Cook for about 2 minutes until the sauce has thickened then pour over the duck breasts.
TO SERVE: accompany with boiled long-grain and wild rice mix, and a chicory and watercress salad. The rice mixture is available in boxes from supermarkets. Allow 50-75g (2-3oz) per serving and cook according to instructions. Stir in 15g (½oz) toasted pine nuts. To toast, shake in a dry frying pan over gentle heat for 1-2 minutes until golden. Dress salad with a vinaigrette dressing.

CHOCOLATE AND CHESTNUT WHIP

A truly luxurious dessert with the rich taste of chocolate, fine texture of chestnuts and luxury of Grand Marnier liqueur.
Serves 2
345 Calories a portion

50g (2oz) plain chocolate, broken into pieces
60ml (2fl oz) single cream
100g (4oz) unsweetened chestnut purée (See Cook's Note)
1 tbsp Grand Marnier liqueur
2 chocolate leaves, to decorate
brandy snaps, to serve

Melt the chocolate with all but a tablespoon of the cream in a small saucepan over a gentle heat. Place in a food processor or blender with the chestnut purée and the liqueur and blend until smooth. Spoon into 2 glasses and swirl in the remaining cream. Decorate with a chocolate leaf. Serve with brandy snaps.

COOK'S NOTE
Chestnut purée only comes in large cans so you'll have some left over. Freeze the remainder in a rigid container and use at a later date for a savoury stuffing or a dessert. It will keep frozen for up to 6 months.

WINE CHOICE
Try a spicy white wine such as Alsace Gewürztraminer or Hungarian Tokay; or if you prefer red, go for something like an Australian Cabernet Sauvignon. Failing these, saki would be a good choice. This is a dry rice wine and should be served warm. You can buy special warmers from some off-licences, otherwise warm gently in a pan. Pour into a jug ready to serve.

ROMANTIC DINNER FOR TWO

A special meal that's sure to impress

Avocado and Prawn Salad

Chicken in Raspberry Sauce

New Potatoes with Sweetcorn and French Beans

Peach and Passion Fruit Fool

A stunning romantic dinner – serve with a glass of pink champagne

TIMEPLAN FOR SERVING DINNER AT 8.00PM

7.30 *Prepare the Peach and Passion Fruit Fool. Chill. (Thaw prawns in cold water if necessary.)*
7.40 *Start to cook chicken breasts and prepare the vegetables – just wash and trim – although it's very fashionable to leave the tails on French beans!*
7.45 *Put water on to boil for the vegetables. Prepare the avocado and arrange the slices in a fan shape on individual plates.*
7.50 *Put potatoes into boiling water to start cooking. Salt lightly.*

7.55 *Finish preparing the starter then place on the table.*
Place chicken on individual plates and keep warm. Add the sauce ingredients to the pan, blend together then turn off heat. Just before sitting down to eat, add the beans and sweetcorn to the potatoes and leave to cook while eating the first course.
8.00 *Start the meal.*
Reheat the sauce for the chicken and drain the vegetables and toss in butter just before serving.

AVOCADO AND PRAWN SALAD

A special way of serving avocado and prawns – always a popular combination. The avocado doesn't need sprinkling with lemon juice because it's only prepared a very short time before serving and so won't discolour.
Serves 2
310 Calories a portion

1 avocado, ripe but still firm
125g (4oz) peeled prawns
1-2 tbsp mayonnaise
paprika, for sprinkling

Peel, halve and stone the avocado, then slice lengthways. Fan the slices out on one side of each serving plate. Mix the prawns and mayonnaise then spoon on to the plates and sprinkle with paprika.

CHICKEN IN RASPBERRY SAUCE

This tangy fruit sauce also goes rather well with pork escalopes.
Serves 2
390 Calories a portion

25g (1oz) butter
2 tsp oil
2 chicken breasts, weighing about 175g (6oz) each
125g (4oz) raspberries, thawed if frozen
2 tsp arrowroot
150ml (¼ pint) cider
a few sprigs of mint, to garnish

Heat half the butter with the oil in a large non-stick frying pan and add the chicken breasts. Cover and cook over a medium heat for 10-12 minutes, turning them occasionally until evenly browned and cooked through.

Lift the chicken from the pan and place on individual warmed dinner plates. Keep warm. Drain the excess fat from the frying pan, retaining any juices, then add the remaining butter. Reserve 6 nice looking raspberries, then sieve the rest into the pan.

Whisk the arrowroot into the cider and add to the pan. Bring to the boil, stirring until the sauce thickens. When ready to serve, spoon a little sauce over each chicken breast. Serve the remainder separately.

Garnish with raspberries and mint.

NEW POTATOES WITH SWEETCORN AND FRENCH BEANS

Serves 2
185 Calories a portion

Cook 175g (6oz) halved new potatoes in lightly salted water for 7 minutes then add 125g (4oz) whole baby sweetcorn and 75g (3oz) French beans and cook for a further 7-8 minutes until the vegetables are tender. Toss in butter before serving.

PEACH AND PASSION FRUIT FOOL

A melt-in-the-mouth dessert with the combined textures of firm peach and slightly crunchy passion fruit seeds. Use any flavour fromage frais, but if you buy a multi-pack of 4 different flavours, a combination of peach and redcurrant with tropical fruit is really lovely.
Serves 2
180 Calories a portion

1 fresh peach
two 100g (3.½oz) pots plain or fruit flavoured fromage frais
2 passion fruit
4 tsp demerara sugar
¼ tsp ground cinnamon
almond tuiles biscuits, for serving

Stone and dice the peach then mix three quarters in a bowl with the fromage frais. Cut the passion fruit in half, scoop out the seeds and add to the peach mixture with half the sugar. Spoon into two sundae or wine glasses. Top with the reserved peach then sprinkle with the remaining sugar and cinnamon. Chill until ready to serve.

Serve with almond tuiles biscuits.

WINE CHOICE
Pink champagne is delightfully indulgent if price is no object; but 'blush' wine, although just a Californian rosé by another name, seems to be made for this occasion too; it sometimes goes under the exotic, if perverse, name White Zinfandel. St Amour is a special occasion Beaujolais – 1985 is good – and some lucky people claim that red Burgundy is an aphrodisiac! Finish with half a bottle of one of the German Spätlese dessert wines.

Avocado and Prawn Salad

A NEW YEAR'S EVE SUPPER FOR TEN

See the New Year in with friends with this delicious Indian-style meal for ten

Tandoori Spiced Chicken

Fruit and Nut Pilau

Cucumber and Kiwi Salad

Pappads with mango chutney

Exotic Fruits

COOK'S NOTE
Tandoori paste is available from large supermarkets and Indian grocers. It's a mixture of Indian spices, seasoning and garlic, which is ready to use, unlike Tandoori spice mixture in powder form which needs additional ingredients.

DRINKS CHOICE
Chilled beer or lager would be most refreshing with this meal or, if you prefer to drink wine, go for a full-bodied spicy wine, such as an Alsace Gewürztraminer. This wine has a heady, almost perfumed scent and rather exotic taste which would stand up well to the spices and make an excellent choice. A very cold medium-sweet white wine would also be suitable. Try an inexpensive Liebfraumilch or a still or sparkling Vouvray from the Loire Valley.

Clockwise from left, Fruit and Nut Pilau, Tandoori Spiced Chicken, Pappads and Cucumber and Kiwi Salad

TIMEPLAN FOR SERVING SUPPER AT 10.00PM

9.30 Put a full kettle of water on to boil. Prepare the Tandoori Spiced Chicken and bake on the top shelf of a preheated oven at 230°C (450°F) gas 8 for 20 minutes.

9.38 Spread the pappads from two 128g (4.½oz) packets on to baking sheets and bake in the oven for 10 minutes.

9.40 Thoroughly wash the rice then put on to cook using the boiled water from the kettle. Add the stock cubes, apricots, turmeric and seasoning then boil rapidly for 5 minutes.

9.48 Remove the pappads from the oven and arrange in a basket.

9.50 Dice the cucumber and place in a serving bowl with the mint sauce and seasoning.

9.53 Turn off the rice and leave to continue cooking.

9.54 Peel and slice the kiwi fruit then mix into the cucumber mixture.

9.58 Shred the lettuce and place on a large serving platter for the chicken. Tip a jar of mango chutney into a serving dish and garnish with coriander. Add the dates and nuts to the cooked rice.

10.00 Dish up the chicken and rice. Stir the yogurt into the chicken juices and serve separately.

TANDOORI SPICED CHICKEN

This is quick to prepare and cooks without attention while you prepare the rice, salad and pappads.
Serves 10
300 Calories a portion

2kg (4.½lb) skinned boneless chicken breasts
1 large onion, sliced
5 tbsp Tandoori paste (see Cook's Note)
1 tbsp each ground coriander and cumin
4 tbsp oil
TO SERVE:
1 iceberg lettuce
5 tbsp Greek yogurt
fresh coriander, to garnish

Cut each chicken breast into 4 with a sharp knife then place in a bowl with the onion, Tandoori paste and spices and mix well.

Pour the oil into a large roasting tin then swirl it round so that the base is covered. Tip in the chicken and onion mixture then bake at 230°C (450°F) gas 8 for 20-25 minutes, or until the chicken is tender.

Meanwhile shred the lettuce and place on one large or divide between 2 smaller platters.

Spoon the cooked chicken and onion mixture on top. Add the yogurt to the pan juices and serve separately. Garnish with coriander.

FRUIT AND NUT PILAU

Instead of serving plain boiled rice try this golden-coloured pilau that contains nuts, apricots and dates.
Serves 10
335 Calories a portion

750g (1.½lb) basmati rice
1.½litres (3pints) boiling water
3 chicken stock cubes
1 tbsp ground turmeric
250g (8oz) no-need-to-soak dried apricots
½ tsp salt
freshly ground black pepper
125g (4oz) dried stoned dates
50g (2oz) salted peanuts

Wash and drain the rice to remove the excess starch. Place in a large saucepan then pour over the boiling water. Add the stock cubes, turmeric, apricots and seasoning then bring to the boil and boil rapidly for 5 minutes. Turn off the heat and cover – while standing the rice will continue to cook and absorb the excess liquid. Stir in the dates and peanuts just before serving.

CUCUMBER AND KIWI SALAD

Use ready-made mint sauce for this refreshing salad of cucumber and kiwi fruit. Slices of banana tossed in lemon juice and toasted cumin seeds also make a good accompaniment to spicy foods.
Serves 10
20 Calories a portion

1.½ cucumbers, diced
5 kiwi fruit, peeled and sliced
1.½ tsp mint sauce
salt and freshly ground black pepper

Place the prepared fruit in a serving bowl with the mint and seasoning and mix well. Serve chilled.

PAPPADS

Bombay spiced pappads, available from large supermarkets and Indian grocers, are thick poppadoms for grilling or baking rather than frying.

EXOTIC FRUITS

Buy a selection of exotic fresh fruits such as those shown below – lychees, kumquats, passion fruit, mangoes, pomegranates, prickly pears, figs and star fruit. Arrange in advance on decorative platters with shortbread petticoat tails.

Exotic Fruits

AN INFORMAL SUPPER FOR TWELVE

An easy, economical meal for a crowd

*Spicy Mince Tacos with
Cheese and Salad*

*Blackberry Meringue
Crush*

TIMEPLAN FOR SERVING SUPPER AT 8.00PM

7.30 Put all the ingredients for the spicy mince in a very large pan and bring to the boil. Turn down the heat and leave to simmer. Stir occasionally, until ready to serve.

7.35 Make and decorate the Blackberry Meringue Crush, then chill until ready to serve.

7.45 Put the tacos in the oven at 150°C (300°F) gas 2 to heat through. Meanwhile, grate the cheese, chop the salad ingredients and pile each into a different bowl. Put the spicy mince in a large

8.00 bowl, place on a large platter and surround with the tacos. Serve with the salad, cheese and chilli relish. Serve the dessert when you are ready.

COOK'S NOTE
Tacos are crispy Mexican shells, made from unrefined cornflour, which can be filled with different ingredients and eaten with your fingers. They are widely available from supermarkets. Alternatively use warm mini pitta breads instead.

WINE CHOICE
Litre bottles of Liebfraumilch would be a good choice to serve for a crowd and flatter the spiciness of the tacos. Alternatively, to keep both price and alcohol low, serve Sangria wine (red or white), diluted with sparkling mineral water and chopped fresh fruit. Add plenty of ice cubes and, if liked, a glass of brandy. Both of these will go equally well with the dessert.

Spicy Mince Tacos with Cheese and Salad

SPICY MINCE TACOS

These make a tasty, informal meal and are so simple to serve. Just lay out on the table the spicy mince, chopped salad vegetables, grated cheese and relish, then guests can put together their own tacos and eat at their leisure.
Makes 24
335 Calories a portion

SPICY MINCE:
2kg (4lb) extra lean minced beef
800g (1lb 12oz) can tomatoes
4 tbsp tomato purée
4 beef stock cubes
2 tbsp ground paprika
2 tbsp ground cumin
1 tbsp dried oregano
250g (8oz) mixed, dried fruit
3 tbsp plain flour
TO SERVE:
24 taco shells (see Cook's Note)
1 frisée (curly endive) or iceberg lettuce, shredded
2 bunches spring onions, trimmed and chopped
3 avocados, peeled and sliced
375g (12oz) Cheddar cheese, grated
1 large jar chilli relish

Put all the spicy mince ingredients into a very large pan. Stir thoroughly then bring to the boil, cover and simmer gently for 25 minutes.

Meanwhile, prepare the salad vegetables and put into bowls with the cheese and chilli relish. Ten minutes before you are ready to serve, heat the tacos at 150°C (300°F) gas 2.
TO SERVE: allow each guest to help themselves, first putting a tablespoon or two of the mince into the taco shell then topping with the salad, cheese and relish if liked.

Blackberries and meringue – a delicious combination

BLACKBERRY MERINGUE CRUSH

This dessert can be made using any soft fruit – simply match the fruit with the jam. Don't add the meringues too far in advance as they will start to dissolve.
Serves 12
330 Calories a portion

600ml (1pint) double cream
6 tbsp blackberry jam or jelly
1kg (2lb) fromage frais
1kg (2lb) prepared blackberries, thawed if frozen
6 bought meringue nests, broken fresh blackberry leaves, to decorate (optional)

Beat the cream and blackberry jam or jelly, preferably in a mixer, until very thick. Fold in the fromage frais, half of the blackberries and the broken meringues. Divide between 2 large glass serving dishes and decorate with the remaining blackberries and fresh leaves, if using

INDEX

Almond stuffed peaches 89
American-style summer lunch 42-3
Apricot and almond ambrosia 55
Apricot and cardamom compote 61
Avocado and prawn salad 104
Avocado, watercress and tomato salad 51

Bakery selection with lemony and
  cranberry toppings 97
Banana:
    Banana coffee creams 91
    Bananas Barbados 99
    Caribbean bananas 9
Beef:
    Spicy mince tacos 109
    Stir-fried beef in black bean sauce 77
Blackberry meringue crush 109
Blackberry and strawberry shortcake 42
Blackcurrant and raspberry refresher 20

Cabbage:
    Summer cabbage 10
Caribbean supper 78-9
Carrots, buttered 92
Celebration dinner for two 102-3
Cheese:
    Cheese and apple scramble 97
    Cheese and leek ramekins 36
    Cheese mash 65
    French cheese platter with fruit 44
Cherry croissants 46
Cherry and plum meringue 49
Chicken:
    Chicken with almonds and raisins 91
    Chicken with lime and thyme 9
    Chicken and raspberry salad 46
    Chicken in raspberry sauce 105
    Hot chicken and bacon salad 42
    Lemon and coriander chicken 80
    Normandy chicken 87
    Sesame spiced chicken 51
    Tandoori spiced chicken 107
Chinese meal 80-1
Chocolate:
    Chocolate and chestnut whip 103
    Hot chocolate 97
    White chocolate and hazelnut
      creams 100
Citrus, honey and almond salad 32
Clementine brûlée 69
Coconut rice 77
Cod:
    Pizza topped cod 83
Colourful stir-fry supper 20-1
Courgette and basil risotto 32
Courgette and carrot ribbons 16
Courgette salad, hot 61
Creative vegetarian meal for
  four 36-9

Crunchy syrup tartlets 63
Cucumber and kiwi salad 107
Delicious mid-week meal 14-15
Delicious quick meal 98-9
Delicious summer dinner 56-7
Desserts:
    Almond stuffed peaches 89
    Apricot and almond ambrosia 55
    Apricot and cardamom compote 61
    Baked figs with ginger honey 31
    Banana coffee creams 91
    Bananas Barbados 99
    Blackberry meringue crush 109
    Blackberry and strawberry shortcake 42
    Caribbean bananas 9
    Cherry croissants 46
    Cherry and plum meringue 49
    Chocolate and chestnut whip 103
    Citrus, honey and almond salad 32
    Clementine brûlée 69
    Crunchy syrup tartlets 63
    Exotic fruit and chocolate platter 25
    Exotic fruits 107
    Fresh mango 28
    Fruit creation 78
    Fruit and nut peaches 15
    Gooseberry bramble with sorbet 87
    Lemon and hazelnut ice with honey 56
    Liqueur strawberries 40
    Melon and mango with Cointreau 35
    Mocha cream 18
    Nectarine Cointreau surprise 95
    Peach and passion fruit fool 105
    Peaches with passion fruit 26
    Pears with hot ginger sauce 85
    Pineapple almondine 83
    Plum and almond crumble 70
    Plums in red wine 10
    Raspberry ratafia crush 75
    Rhubarb and ginger fool 59
    Rhubarb and raspberry kissel 23
    Salad of exotic fruits 16
    Spiced fruit compote 39
    Strawberries cassis 51
    Strawberry caramel cream 52
    Sunshine salad 72
    Three-fruit salad with ginger 77
    Vanilla ice with blackberry and
      passion fruit sauce 80
    White chocolate and hazelnut
      creams 100
Duck breasts with kumquats 103

Easy vegetarian dinner 40-1
Egg:
    Cheese and apple scramble 97
    Eggs with spicy sauce 28
Exotic family meal 90-1

Figs, baked, with ginger honey 31
French beans, herby 65

French-style dinner for four 86-7
French-style peas 95
Frisée salad 78
Fruit. See also Apricot etc.
    Exotic fruit and chocolate platter 25
    Exotic fruits with petticoat tails 107
    Fruit creation 78
    Fruit and nut peaches 15
    Fruit and nut pilau 107
    Salad of exotic fruits 16
    Spiced fruit compote 39
    Three-fruit salad with ginger 77

Garlic grilled tomatoes 70
Garlic rolls, fresh baked 52
Garlic vegetable medley 9
Gooseberry bramble with sorbet 87
Grapefruit Miller Howe 97
Green leaf salad 32

Haddock:
    Haddock florentine 63
    Haddock julienne 55
    Lemon glazed haddock with caper
      sauce 72
Hash browns 70
Hearty family supper 64-5
Herby French beans 65

Iceberg salad with hot walnut dressing 59
Impressive quick meal 92-3
Informal meal with friends 100-1
Informal supper for twelve 108-9
Italian meal for four 88-9
Italian-style vegetarian meal 30-1

Lamb:
    Barbecued lamb and pepper kebabs 56
    Lamb and apricot sauté 20
    Lamb cutlets with sultana and
      ginger pilaf 100
    Lamb and leek stir-fry 85
    Lamb with mint and cranberry glaze 92
    Lamb with tomatoes 61
    Minty orange lamb chops 16
Leaf and Nut Salad 26
Leek:
    Cheese and leek ramekins 36
    Shredded leeks with poppy seeds 92
Lemon and coriander chicken 80
Lemon glazed haddock with caper
  sauce 72
Lemon and hazelnut ice with honey 56
Lemony rice 91
Light summer meal 46-7
Liqueur strawberries 40
Low-calorie lunch for four 54-5

Mango:
    Fresh mango 28
    Fruit creation 78

Melon and mango with Cointreau 35
Microwave meal 10-11
Minty orange lamb chops 16
Mixed leaf salad 26,66
Mixed leaf salad with hazelnut dressing 31
Mocha cream 18
Monkfish with mustard butter sauce 10
Mushroom:
    Hot marinated mushrooms 36
    Stuffed mushrooms en croûte 10

Nectarine Cointreau surprise 95
New Year's Eve supper for ten 106-7
Noodles:
    Ribbon noodles with thyme 15
    Sesame noodles 80

Orange and coriander rice 55
Oriental meal 76-7
Outdoor summer supper 52-3

Parma ham with melon 88
Parmentier potatoes 63
Parmesan potatoes 69
Pasta. *See also* Tagliatelle
    Buttered pasta 22
    Pasta with creamy vegetable medley 31
    Pasta paprika 99
    Pasta and pepper salad 49
    Pasta pomodoro 35
    Pasta with tuna and mushrooms 89
Peach:
    Almond stuffed peaches 89
    Fruit and nut peaches 15
    Peach and passion fruit fool 105
    Peaches with passion fruit 26
Pears with hot ginger sauce 85
Peas with lettuce and spring onions 75
Pesto, bread, hot 66
Petits pois à la française 99
Pineapple almondine 83
Pistou 44
Pizza topped cod 83
Plum and almond crumble 70
Plums in red wine 10
Pork:
    Escalopes with creamy mushroom
      sauce 99
    Pork argenteuil 22
    Pork and sage burgers 12
    Pork with sage and mustard 75
    Pork with stroganoff sauce 15
Potato:
    Cheese mash 65
    Hash browns 70
    Hot new potatoes 10
    Hot potato salad 25
    New potatoes with sweetcorn and
      French beans 105
    Parmentier potatoes 63
    Parmesan potatoes 69

Peppered new potatoes 51
Potato and sprout purée with
  cheese and nutmeg 92
Sesame potatoes 95
Sesame potatoes with chives 61
Spicy seeded potatoes 85
Prawns in creole sauce 78

Quick Italian meal 34-5
Quick tasty supper 66-7

Radicchio and frisée salad 35
Raspberry:
    Blackcurrant and raspberry refresher 20
    Chicken and raspberry salad 46
    Chicken in raspberry sauce 105
    Raspberry ratafia crush 75
    Relaxed summer lunch 50-1
Rhubarb and ginger fool 59
Rhubarb and raspberry kissel 23
Rice:
    Coconut rice 77
    Courgette and basil risotto 32
    Fruit and nut pilau 107
    Lemony rice 91
    Orange and coriander rice 55
    Saffron and seafood rice 59
    Tomato and tuna risotto 66
Romantic dinner for two 104-5

Saffron and seafood rice 59
Salads. *For fruit salads see* Desserts
    Avocado and prawn salad 104
    Avocado, watercress and tomato
      salad 51
    Cucumber and kiwi salad 107
    Frisée salad 78
    Green leaf salad 32
    Hot chicken and bacon salad 42
    Hot courgette salad 61
    Hot potato salad 25
    Iceberg salad with hot walnut dressing 59
    Leaf and nut salad 26
    Mixed leaf salad 66
    Mixed leaf salad with hazelnut
      dressing 31
    Pasta and pepper salad 49
    Radicchio and frisée salad 35
    Salad Italian style 83
    Salad of leaves 40
    Tabbouleh 56
Saturday snack 12-13
Saturday soup 12
Sausage:
    Somerset sausage hotpot 65
Sesame noodles 80
Sesame spiced chicken 51
Sesame potatoes 95
Sesame vegetables 28
Simple fish supper 72-3
Simple Italian-style supper 82-3

Simple oven-baked supper 62-3
Simple Provence-style supper 44-5
Soup:
    Pistou 44
    Saturday soup 12
Special family meal 24-5
Special Friday supper 58-9
Special occasion brunch 96-7
Special turkey meal 94-5
Speedy family supper 74-5
Speedy mid-week meal 18-19
Speedy vegetarian supper 32-3
Spicy vegetarian supper 28-9
Springtime dinner for four 22-3
Steaks with peppercorn sauce 25
Strawberry:
    Liqueur strawberries 40
    Strawberries cassis 51
    Strawberry caramel cream 52
    Strawberry and passion fruit milk
      shake 97
Stunning stir-fry 84-5
Summer cabbage 10
Summer niçoise 52
Summertime supper 48-9
Sunshine salad 72

Tabbouleh 56
Tagliatelle with courgettes and
  lemon cream 40
Tagliatelle, fresh, with cheese and
  tomato sauce 26
Tandoori spiced chicken 107
Tasty lamb dinner 16-17
Tasty mid-week supper 60-1
Tomato:
    Garlic grilled tomatoes 70
    Thyme baked tomatoes 63
    Tomato and cucumber vinaigrette 91
    Tomato and tuna risotto 66
    Tomatoes with green onions 39
Trout with tartare butter 18
Tuna:
Pasta with tuna and mushrooms 89
    Tomato and tuna risotto 66
Turkey with tarragon sauce 95
Turkey feast supper 68-9

Vanilla ice with blackberry and
  passion fruit sauce 80
Vegetable. *See also* Cabbage etc.
    Braised mixed vegetables 18
    Garlic vegetables medley 9
    Pistou 44
    Saturday soup 12
    Sesame vegetables 28
    Steamed vegetable medley 100
    Vegetable and turkey fricassée 69
Vegetarian lunch 26-7

Warming winter meal 8-9

Acknowledgements

The Publishers and Living would like to thank the following individuals
who were involved in the preparation of material for this book:

Special Photography: David Armstrong page 64; Nick Carman pages 104-5;
James Duncan pages 22-3 and 86-7; Laurie Evans pages 14, 19, 37-8 and 82;
Ken Field pages 53, 58, 60 and 68; James Jackson pages 81 and 88-9;
David Gill pages 11 and 101; Paul Grater pages 62, 66, 76 and 98;
Graham Kirk pages 8, 17, 21, 24, 27, 29-30, 34, 41, 43, 48, 50, 57, 74, 84, 90,
93, 96 and 102; Chris Knaggs 45 and 79
and Alan Newnham pages 13, 54-5, 71, 73, 94, and 106-109.

Sara Buenfeld would like to thank her cookery team,
Maggie Mayhew and Iris Harvey and Living's Art Director Julia Boulton
as well as guest contributors, especially Sarah Brown, Sara Lewis,
Kate Moseley, Maggie Pannell and Catherine Readington.